Chachapoya Textiles

CMA 845. Photo: Adriana von Hagen.

Chachapoya Textiles

The Laguna de los Cóndores Textiles
in the Museo Leymebamba, Chachapoyas, Peru

EDITED BY
LENA BJERREGAARD

WITH THE ASSISTANCE OF
ADRIANA VON HAGEN

—

THE MUSEO LEYMEBAMBA TEXTILE CATALOGUE
BY LENA BJERREGAARD

MUSEUM TUSCULANUM PRESS
UNIVERSITY OF COPENHAGEN 2007

Lena Bjerregaard (ed.): *Chachapoya Textiles*

© Museum Tusculanum Press and the authors, 2007
Consultants: Elena Phipps, Conservator in the Department of Textile Conservation at the Metropolitan Museum of Art, New York, and Ivan Boserup, The Royal Library, Copenhagen
Copy editor: Pernille Flensted Jensen
Cover, layout and composition: Pernille Sys Hansen
Set in Quadraat and Quadraat sans
Printed by Narayana Press, narayanapress.dk
ISBN 978 87 635 0499 7

Cover photo: Lena Bjerregaard. See pp. 12-15

All drawings from R. d'Harcourt: *Textiles of Ancient Peru and their Techniques*, University of Washington Press, Seattle, 1975, are reprinted by permission of the University of Washington Press

This catalogue is published with the financial support from
Augustinus Fonden
The Danish Research Council for the Humanities
Højesteretssagfører C.L.Davids Fond for Slægt og Venner
Landsdommer V. Gieses Legat
Lillian og Dan Finks Fond
Novo Nordisk Fonden
Dronning Margrethe og Prins Henriks Fond

Museum Tusculanum Press
Njalsgade 126
DK–2300 Copenhagen S
www.mtp.dk

Contents

Lena Bjerregaard / Adriana von Hagen
The Museo Leymebamba Textile Collection — 9

Inge Schjellerup
Placing the Chachapoya and the Inkas on the Map — 17

Sonia Guillén
Preserving the Heritage of the Chachapoya
THE MUSEO LEYMEBAMBA AND THE MUMMIES FROM LAGUNA DE LOS CÓNDORES — 23

Lena Bjerregaard
Textiles, Materials and Technologies — 29

Adriana von Hagen
Stylistic Influences and Imagery in the Museo Leymebamba Textiles — 41

Gary Urton
The Khipus from Laguna de los Cóndores — 63

Lena Bjerregaard
The Museo Leymebamba Textile Catalogue — 69

Bibliography — 111

The Authors — 115

Acknowledgements

The research for this catalogue was financed by The Foundation for Research and Conservation of Andean Monuments.

This catalogue has been financed by Augustinus Fonden, The Danish Research Council for the Humanities, Højesteretssagfører C.L.Davids Fond for Slægt og Venner, Landsdommer V. Gieses Legat, Lillian og Dan Finks Fond, Novo Nordisk Fonden, and Dronning Margrethe og Prins Henriks Fond.

I want to thank Adriana von Hagen for the huge editorial work she did on this book.

In memory of Ann Paul, who was a great inspiration.

Lena Bjerregaard

LENA BJERREGAARD / ADRIANA VON HAGEN

The Museo Leymebamba Textile Collection

INTRODUCTION

This catalogue analyzes some of the most unusual and representative textiles – burial offerings and mummy bundle wrappings – discovered in 1996 at a cliffside burial site overlooking Laguna de los Cóndores in the cloud forest of the northern Peruvian Andes. The finds include the best preserved and largest cache of Chachapoya[1] textiles known to date, providing researchers with a unique opportunity to learn about little-known Chachapoya weaving technology and style. Because the site had been looted, many of the textiles were scattered in and around the tombs, or *chullpas*, (above-ground burial structures). Others have been removed from mummy bundles as part of ongoing conservation at the Museo

View of Laguna de los Cóndores. Photo: Adriana von Hagen.

San Antonio, Chachapoya. Unexcavated Chachapoya site with walls and round house mounts. Photo: Lena Bjerregaard.

Leymebamba, where the textiles are either stored or exhibited. Most of the textiles date to the Chachapoya-Inka period, ca. 1470–1532, although some may have been produced earlier or may date to Spanish Colonial times. The styles include local Chachapoya, Chachapoya-Inka, provincial Inka and imports from the coast or the tropical lowlands.

The ancient Chachapoya once held sway over a vast territory in the northern Peruvian Andes, bordered by the Marañón river to the west and the Huallaga river to the east. Today the region is scattered with the distinctive remains of their trademark cliff tombs and hamlets of circular structures. Feared warriors and famed shamans, the Chachapoya flourished from around AD 800 until their violent conquest by the Inkas in the 1470s. The arrival of the Spaniards in the 1530s spelled the end of the Inka empire, and brought renewed hardship to the Chachapoya as the conquistadors systematically seized their land and imposed forced labor and tribute burdens on native peoples. More recently, looters and vandals have engaged archaeologists in a desperate race to save the remains of this little-known civilization.

Despite over a century of exploration and more recent archaeological and archival research, our understanding of Chachapoya prehistory remains fragmentary. "Classic" Chachapoya civilization – with its hallmark circular constructions and masonry friezes – appears to have coalesced around AD 800 and continued into Inka times, ca. 1470–1532.

Like the culture itself, the Chachapoya art style

Cuélap, the largest excavated Chachapoya site. Photo: Adriana von Hagen.

Double zig-zag frieze at the Chachapoya site of San Antonio, in the province of Luya, near Leymebamba. Photo: Adriana von Hagen.

reflects a mix of local and exotic influences. The well-preserved burial offerings from the Laguna de los Cóndores are playing a vital part in finding answers to the genesis of the style, revealing new imagery on perishable artifacts, especially textiles. The Spanish cronicler Pedro Cieza de León writes in his *Crónicas del Péru* in 1553 that the Chachapoya "were making fine and valuable textiles for the Inkas; and still today (1553) they produce wonderful clothing and blankets, so fine and beautiful, that they are highly estimated by everyone".

The textiles from Laguna de los Cóndores bear witness to the skill of the Chachapoya weavers, not only in the art and technology of cloth manufacture but also in the distinct imagery decorating the weavings.

THE BURIAL SITE

Composed of six intact *chullpas* and the foundations of a seventh, the burial site, known as Laguna de los Cóndores 1 or LC1, is one of 18 funerary sites documented on the limestone cliffs looming above Laguna de los Cóndores. The *chullpas'* builders took advantage of a natural ledge, 45 meters long and 5 meters wide, in the limestone cliff. The tombs are nestled against the cliff, which serves as their back wall. The builders modified the ledge by leveling the floor and carving smaller ledges into the cliff onto which they built low masonry walls set in mud mortar that supported the back roofs of the *chullpas*. The roofs are composed of thick, roughly-hewn wooden planks. Each tomb is about 3 meters high and divided into two levels by a platform of small logs. The structures are roughly quadrangular in shape and built of limestone blocks set in mud mortar. Four of them are plastered and painted in shades of white as well as in red and yellow ochre, while zigzag friezes adorn another two. Deer antlers protruded from either side of the window of one *chullpa*. All the *chullpas* face the lake and the ancient settlement of Llaqtacocha, where archaeologists documented some 130 stone structures, mostly circular.

More than 200 mummies, as well as disarticulated skeletons and their burial offerings were placed in the *chullpas*. Unfortunately, the looters who discovered the burial site ransacked the remains, slashing mummy bundles with machetes and pocketing many of the offerings before archaeologists reached the site in July 1997. Nonetheless, the extraordinary preservation of the human and other organic remains is as astonishing as the discovery itself. The skin on the mummies appears supple, the baskets and the decorated gourds look as if they have been made recently, not 500 years ago, and many of the textiles, although somewhat brittle, retain their brilliant colors. What could account for such preservation in an area where rainfall ranges from 2,000 to 4,000mm a year?

In spite of the rainy climate and the water which often falls in sheets from the overhang protecting the *chullpas*, the dry ledge where the *chullpas* are located harbors a dry, cold and stable microclimate that contributed to the preservation of the organic remains. The fibers found in the Laguna de los Cóndores textiles include camelid fiber, cotton and human hair. The protein fibers are much more brittle than the plant fibers and could suggest alkaline conditions. Nonetheless, pH tests with a microelectrode in a controlled water solution indicate that this was not the case. All the tested fibers (10 samples) had a pH between 5 and 6 (slightly acidic); the protein fibers were slightly more acidic than the plant fibers.

Preliminary studies point to the skill of the Laguna de los Cóndores embalmers. The skin of the mummies has been treated and appears leathery, while unspun cotton placed under the cheeks, in the mouth and in the nostrils, preserved facial features. The embalmers controlled decomposition process by emptying the abdominal cavity through the anus, sealing the orifice with a

All mummies are adorned with an embroidered, stylized face and have a braid of hair and cotton yarns protruding from the top of the mummy bundle. For transport from Laguna de los Cóndores to Leymebamba they were wrapped in cotton cloth, and in the museum this is changed into a protective wrapping of transparent tulle. Photo: Lena Bjerregaard.

The storage room for the mummies in the Museo Leymebamba has controlled light and humidity. It can be viewed by the public for only short intervals of time. Photo: Lena Bjerregaard.

cloth plug. Despite these measures, however, the presence of fly pupae in the mummy bundles indicates that there was considerable decay.

Chromatographic studies from the mummy textile fibres made by Jürgen Schram at the Umweltschutzanalytik dept. of the Hochschule Niederrhein/Krefeld/Germany, however, shows a considerable amount of sulfur as sulfite (SO_3^{2-}) (up to 8 w-% in many of the textiles). A small amount of sulfate SO_4^{2-} and traces of $S_2O_3^{2-}$ were also found. This suggests that sulfur may have been burned and the sulfur dioxide SO_2 was through the smoke applied to the mummy textiles as a gas. However, SO_2 has also been used for bleaching textiles in other parts of the world, and further tests have to be made on the mummies themselves before it is possible to prove that sulfur was used as a mummifying agent. Sulfur is, however, a great preservative and may have been applied to the mummies for conservation.

The Analysis

The textiles represent a wide range of objects, including tunics, mantles, bags, bands, belts, nets, headbands, *tupu* cords, interwoven sticks, slings and a possible whip. The techniques used to fashion these objects comprise weaving, looping, braiding, knotting, wrapping and cut pile. The various weaving techniques employed included balanced plain-weave, warp-faced plain-weave, discontinuous warp, complementary warp weave, supplementary, floating weave, tapestry, brocade and tubular weave. Various techniques were used to decorate the cloth: embroidery, tie-dye, tassels and decorative edgings such as woven bands sewn into the edge of the textile selvedge during weaving, stem-stitch embroidery, loop-stitch embroidery and figure-eight stitching.

Many of the textiles show Inka, provincial Inka or Chachapoya traits while others are a mix of styles. (Often, an Inka-style tunic is decorated with Chachapoya-style imagery; see essay by Adriana von Hagen, this volume, for a discussion of Chachapoya iconography). The majority of the Leymebamba tunics have Inka dimensions; that is, they are longer than they are wide. Tunic INCL 111 (p. 84) was woven on an upright loom with a (when on the loom) horizontal warp. The technique employed is tapestry with a cotton warp and camelid fiber weft. The overall effect of the design is checkerboard, and the pattern units contain human and feline heads that are quintessentially Chachapoya in style. Tunic CMA 756 (p. 80) was also woven as one piece, but its warp is vertical and it was created on a backstrap loom as was the rest of the collection. CMA 756, on the other hand, is fashioned in plain-weave cotton and decorated with painted Chachapoya-style anthropomorphic figures. Other tunics were assembled by stitching together two panels along the center and the sides. Three of the tunics are divided into four squares of dark and light cotton on both sides. These are embellished by waistbands and lower edges decorated in a variety of techniques. The complementary warp *chuspa* (coca bag) straps (tubular weaves) are Inka in style (see, for example CMA 671, p. 103), while other bags are executed in tapestry weave and decorated, for instance, with classic Chachapoya images of men with splayed arms and legs and sporting plumed headgear (CMA 834, p. 100).

The collection also contains a large carrying net (INCL 96, p. 109), composed of plaited camelid fiber braids and human hair. Similar nets excavated by Max Uhle in the late nineteenth century at Pachacamac and housed in Berlin's Ethnologisches Museum suggest that the use of human hair to fashion coarse nets is not unusual. Probably the use of human hair, which is a thick fiber, strengthens the object.

Another striking garment is CMA 600 (p. 86), composed of narrow bands (3.5–4.5cm and 19cm wide) woven in plain weave in various colors; two of the bands are tie-dyed. Mantles assembled in a similar fashion and said to come from Ancón and Paramonga are part of the Ethnologisches Museum's collection. The Berlin mantles have parts of bands stitched on crosswise to the first bands and a warp striped 5–7cm-wide edging. The largest Berlin example measures 155 (incomplete) × 137cm, and the Leymebamba fragments may well have formed part of similarly-sized textile.

Two interesting simili velour headbands form part of the Museo Leymebamba collection. One is made of red camelid fiber (similar in technique to one displayed at the American Museum of Natural History in New York; see illustration in Morris and von Hagen 1993: 176, plate 165) while the other is made of black human hair (similar in technique to a camelid fiber headband in the Ethnologisches Museum, Berlin (V A 42247)). Another headband is woven in tapestry and embellished with appliquéd round, white shell beads.

Several mantles, many of which formed the outermost textiles of mummy bundles, have striped cotton warps and wefts with floating supplementary warps that are sometimes discontinuous (e.g. CMA 2069, p. 72). Similar, allthough much more simple, cotton weavings with floating warps are still produced in the area, although not very frequently and the floating warps are not discontinuous. The archaeological examples, however, are unusual for their colors, especially a deep orange (Chica red) and a yellow ochre, not seen elsewhere in ancient Peruvian weavings (see p. 40 for dye analysis)

Finally, the collection contains a large number of looped plant fiber bags ranging in size from 8 x 10cm to 80 x 72cm.

The majority of the plain-weave cotton textiles are 2/1 (paired warps, single wefts) tabby and the yarns are S-spun. In addition, 2/2 or 1/1 plain-weave cotton cloth was recorded. Paired warps and single wefts are not that frequent in ancient Peru and appear to have been a north coast trait (A.P. Rowe 1984).

All the camelid fiber yarns are Z-spun, 2-ply S as is common throughout the ancient Andes. As noted, the cotton yarns are mainly S-spun which could point to a local spinning source for the cotton, while the camelid yarns were probably made in highland spinning and dyeing centers.

One especially unusual feature of the Museo Leymebamba textiles is that many of them were cut across the warp and then folded and sewn. Apparently such finishing techniques were not permitted by the Inka (or other ancient Andean weavers, for that matter), who favored the more tedious way of producing textiles by weaving all the way to the end of the warp, creating textiles with four selvedges, often with looped warp ends. The Inka imposed strict political control over Chachapoyas (indeed, some of those buried at Laguna de los Cóndores were undoubtedly Inka officials; see essay by Gary Urton, this volume, on the Laguna de los Cóndores khipus, the knotted string recording devices), and no doubt they also regulated weaving. Cut cloth may point to textiles produced for local consumption, although qompi – the finest cloth – was usually reserved for the Inka ruler, his court and select administrators. Perhaps these cut examples were produced after 1535 when Inka influence had begun to wane and the Spaniards began to consolidate their hold over Chachapoyas.

NOTES

1 Throughout this volume we use *Chachapoya* to describe the ancient culture, language and inhabitants of the region, while *Chachapoyas* refers to the territory and modern department capital and province.

Inge Schjellerup

Placing the Chachapoya and the Inkas on the Map

In the fifteenth and sixteenth centuries, the Inka conquered many different ethnic groups scattered across the Andean region. Early Spanish chroniclers described one of these groups as the Chachapoya, who occupied a vast territory in the northern Peruvian Andes.

Bordered to the west by the Marañón river, the northeastern slopes of the Andes rise from 900m to 4500m and drop again towards the east. Today, as in Prehispanic times, the land of the Chachapoya embraced the dry tropical forest along the Marañón and rose to rugged mountains drenched in rain, dense cloud forests, impassable rivers and treacherous bogs. River systems provided access to the upper lowlands of the *ceja de montaña*, or "eyebrow of the jungle" and into the real *selva*, or lowland rain forest.

Between the ninth and fifteenth centuries, this setting provided the backdrop for the development of the resilient and vital Chachapoya culture. Their distinctive architecture featured circular buildings with high, solid foundations; many houses contained small subterranean chambers. Stone cornices protruding from the tops of the bases grace many constructions, while sloping ramps or staircases provided access to raised entrances. Many buildings feature stone friezes composed of zigzags, meanders, rhomboids or staggered squares, suggesting that the Chachapoya used a common sym-

Characteristic Chachapoya stone friezes include rhomboids and step fret motifs. Photo: Inge Schjellerup.

bolic language. They applied similar designs to pottery or embellished textiles with woven or embroidered geometric motifs. These symbols hint at significant ethnic and social values and may have enforced local identity, which the Chachapoya maintained through Inka times.

The Chachapoya located many of their settlements in strategic positions on mountaintops that overlooked communication and transportation routes following rivers and valleys. The settlement pattern reveals a sociopolitical hierarchy that favored high altitude zones and strategically placed localities. The Chachapoya divided their land into chiefdoms of varying sizes; these may reflect sub-groups of the main ethnic group. Kinship ties, political and economic integration, as well as common technological, economic and social solutions to environmental challenges (and no doubt warfare and competition over sparse resources) linked the leading chiefdoms and their sub-groups. Agglomerations of more than 400 house structures are rare, indicating that these sites served as the seats of dominant *kurakas*, or local lords. Beginning around 1470, the Inkas launched their conquest of Chachapoyas, overpowering a series of settlements, which later became part of the Inka province of Chachapoyas (Garcilaso de la Vega [1609] 1979: 296). These included Pías, Condormarca, Cajamarquilla (modern Bolívar), Papamarca, Raymipampa (Leymebamba), Suta and Levanto. The archaeological site of Cuélap with its impressive surrounding wall that rises more than 10m, as well as several decorated circular houses, ranks among the best-known Chachapoya settlements.

Chachapoya burial patterns vary according to which particular chiefdom or sub-group occupied the area. The region of Luya, for example, is known for large

The archaeological site of Cuélap with walls rising to a height of 14m. Photo: Inge Schjellerup.

Sarcophagi composed of cane and mud with masks and skulls at Carajía, in the province of Luya. Photo: Inge Schjellerup.

sarcophagi composed of cane and mud and topped with masks and skulls. Santo Tomás de Quillay, Leymebamba and Chuquibamba, on the other hand, feature cliff tombs consisting of small square chambers perched on narrow ledges under cliff overhangs. Other tomb types include large square chambers painted in tones of red and white and with wooden lintels. Yet, despite their different construction techniques, all burial sites are extremely difficult to access, and many could only have been reached with ropes and ladders.

"These Chachapoya Indians are the whitest and most attractive I have seen anywhere I have been in the Indies," wrote the sixteenth-century Spanish chronicler Pedro Cieza de León, noting that "their women were so beautiful that many of them were chosen to be the wives of the Inkas and the vestals of the temples ... They and their men wear woolen clothing and a headband by which they are known wherever they go" (Cieza 1959 [1553]: 99). Other historical sources described them as strong warriors, skillful herb doctors and sorcerers, as well as expert bridge builders (Calancha 1974 [1638]:384; Villagómez 1919 [1649]:151; Polo de Ondegardo 1916 [1571]: 30). Physical anthropological research has revealed Chachapoya men to be 1.59m in stature and wo-

Doorway at the Inca administrative center of Cochabamba. Photo: Adriana von Hagen.

men 1.46m, with average life spans of 45 years (Schjellerup 1997).

The Inca conquest and occupation brought many changes to Chachapoyas. The Inkas fused smaller, dispersed chiefdoms into larger units. This reshuffling of local power, however, did not stop the Chachapoya from rising up three times against the Inkas. As a result, the Inkas dispatched at least 18 Chachapoya groups as *mitmaq* – colonists – to other parts of the empire (Schjellerup 1997). The Inkas also altered the cultural and sacred landscape, introducing a new religion, ideology, language, settlement patterns and ceramic style. The prevailing Inka architectural style of square and rectangular constructions differed markedly from the round constructions of the Chachapoya.

The overwhelming Inka presence in much of Chachapoyas is surprising. We have encountered several Inka sites ranging from the highland administrative

Still hidden Inca sites in the dense forests on the eastern slopes of the Andes. Photo: Inge Schjellerup.

center of Cochabamba, as well as south of Laguna de los Cóndores, and towards the east into the high jungle, or *selva alta*, crossing the eastern *cordillera*. The Inkas located many sites such as *tampus*, or way stations, as well as other installations along Inka roads or at prime agricultural areas in the upper lowlands, where they modified the landscape into terraced mountain slopes. They also situated their settlements at lakes or along streams and springs (Schjellerup 2003).

Long before the Inkas, Andean people viewed water as sacred. This concept appears to have been widespread and shared by many different ethnic groups in some form or another. Thus, the Inkas emphasized water ceremonies because they were imbued with meaning that could readily be understood by many conquered peoples in spite of ethnic or other differences (Sherbondy 1992:53). Springs, rivers and lakes may have pinpointed certain features in the landscape as potential shrine sites important to Inka religion; this may have been one of the reasons that the Inkas reused the Chachapoya burial sites at Laguna de los Cóndores.

In 1532, when the Spaniards occupied Cajamarca in northern Peru and captured the Inka ruler, Atawalpa, Guaman, a Chachapoya *kuraka* or lord, presented himself to the Spanish conquistador Francisco Pizarro. During the civil war between Atawalpa and his half brother, Waskar, the Chachapoya had sided with Waskar. Atawalpa, however, emerged as victorious and the Inka ruler had summoned Guaman to Cajamarca with several thousand of his people, where they awaited further orders to travel to Ecuador as punishment for their treachery. Guaman, baptized Francisco Pizarro Guaman in honor of the conquistador, represented one of the many subdued ethnic groups that joined the Spaniards against the Inkas. Thus, Pizarro became one of the first Spaniards to hear about Chachapoyas. Only in 1535, however, did the first Spaniard, Captain Alonso de Alvarado, enter Chachapoyas, where Francisco Pizarro Guaman proved enormously helpful.

Although European diseases ravaged at least two-thirds of the Chachapoya population in the Spanish colonial period, we still see traces of the Chachapoya cultural legacy preserved in agricultural practices and in the art of weaving.

Sonia Guillén

Preserving the Heritage of the Chachapoya

The Museo Leymebamba and the Mummies from Laguna de los Cóndores

In late 1996, men working for Julio Ullilén, a cattle rancher from Leymebamba, spotted telltale red paint decorated funerary structures perched on cliffs overlooking Laguna de los Cóndores. Wielding machetes, the ranch hands turned into opportunistic looters, slashing mummy bundles and rummaging through the tombs searching for metal artifacts and other objects they could sell. Before long, the looters began squabbling amongst themselves and eventually the police intervened, arresting most of the looters. Ullilén, in the meantime, had seized much of the looters' booty, which the police confiscated. In April 1997, news of the find caught the attention of the media.

That same month, Peter Lerche, a German-Peruvian anthropologist, visited the remote site. Representing Peru's National Institute of Culture, INC, he led a group that included police and local community members. As the first scientist to reach the isolated burial site he recognized its importance and prepared a preliminary inventory of the find: an estimated 60–70 mummy bundles and hundreds of funerary offerings – pottery, gourds, carved wooden figures, baskets, khipus and much more – strewn chaotically along the narrow ledge that harbored the six tombs. Shortly after Lerche's visit, TV reporter Bibiana Melzi reached the site. Her expedition included people from Leymebamba as well as two Dutch tourists. News of the discovery was already attracting the most adventurous tourists willing to undertake the 10-hour slog on horseback and foot to the lake. Melzi's report became an important resource for archaeologists reconstructing conditions at the site immediately after the looting.

By the time Adriana von Hagen and I arrived in Leymebamba in late May we did not intend to visit the distant lake, we merely wanted to see if the descriptions in the media of mummified human remains were accurate. It was hard to imagine that a cloud forest environment could have conserved the mummies. Furthermore, the association of khipus and mummies, and the possibility that the Laguna de los Cóndores mummies were truly Inka bodies intrigued us.

In Leymebamba, members of the recently created local office of the INC asked us to help them inventory the confiscated artifacts, on display at the municipality. Surprisingly, despite recent visits by archaeologists, nobody had suggested even basic conservation measures and some of the textiles sagged from large, rusty nails tacked to the walls. Judging by the artifacts on display it was clear that the looters had not been able to gain much from selling the pieces. Thus, they opted to transform some of the ancient artifacts into utilitarian objects, converting a gourd into a musical instrument. They also washed a khipu in detergent, fading its colors.

The Leymebamba INC told us that they did not intend to allow any of the materials to leave town. They had prevented archaeologist Federico Kauffmann from taking a mummy bundle to Lima and rejected all requests to send the material to Chachapoyas, the department capi-

Panoramic view of the Museo Leymebamba. Photo: Adriana von Hagen.

tal. Moreover, they indicated that they expected to have a say in all proposals to study the material and that any project should include local people. As director of Centro Mallqui, I was more than eager to explain that their requests coincided fully with the way we conducted research. I did not expect to return to Leymebamba given the difficulty of getting there. At the same time, ongoing work in Ilo, on Peru's far south coast, where Centro Mallqui runs a museum, sponsors excavations and manages a large collection of mummies and grave goods, required me to spend much of my time there.

SALVAGE ARCHAEOLOGY

Nonetheless, it was obvious that the impressive and unique finds could shed great light on the little-known prehistory of the region. I surmised that the mummy bundles might contain well-preserved bodies. Back in Lima, our interest in the collection increased. The possibility of recovering evidence for ancient mummification techniques and elucidating the relationship between the Chachapoya and the conquering Inkas enticed us. Yet the logistical complications of reaching the lake and conducting fieldwork in the cloud forest discouraged us, as did the high cost of conducting such an operation. This marked the onset of a valuable partnership. Adriana von Hagen, a writer who specializes in Andean prehistory, contributed her interest in the environment, a talent for logistics and access to private funds. She became a permanent member of the Leymebamba project, and her studies on the collection are producing valuable insights into regional prehistory.

Meanwhile, Peter Lerche had introduced us to Amy Bucher, a television producer with Engel Brothers Media, a New York documentary film company that had already been considering the possibility of a documentary on the Chachapoya. Through them, we approached the Discovery Channel, which agreed to provide funds to cover fieldwork. Funds from these private sources amounted to over half of the budget for what we envisioned as a short field season.

Because preservation at the site appeared to be good, we designed a program that considered leaving the mummies and offerings at the site. This decision, in part, reflected the lack of adequate facilities in Leymebamba. Our project included cataloging the artifacts and evaluating their conservation conditions, with some on-site emergency treatment. We also expected to collect a sample of diagnostic materials which would join the mummies and artifacts seized from the looters in Leymebamba and which could provide samples for laboratory studies.

The INC evaluated and approved our project, as did the local INC and the community of Leymebamba. In July, we began a three-month program that would provide sufficient time for an emergency evaluation. We contracted Ricardo Morales, an art and architecture conservator, to evaluate the condition of the tombs. His report confirmed that earthquake damage and water seeping through cracks in the overhang, as well as reckless visitors clambering over the fragile structures, were slowly destroying the chambers.

The team at the site included archaeologist Mónica Panaifo, our field director; Adriana von Hagen; Peter Lerche; photographer Ron Wagter; four young archaeology students from San Marcos University (three of whom came from Chachapoyas); a representative of the local INC and members of the community serving as field assistants and muleteers.

Despite the constant rain and damp cold, the location was spectacular and the surroundings breathtaking. Moreover, despite the cattle roaming through large swathes of deforested land, some areas surrounding the lake were still pristine. Remains of a residential site, which we named Llaqtacocha, sprawled along the moraine on the north side of the lake, across from the tombs.

The negative impact of tourism soon became apparent. Visitors often moved mummies to pose them for cameras and they pocketed souvenirs. Rodents used the site as dens or gnawed on exposed bones. As work progressed we realized that the collection was much larger than we had anticipated; our original estimate of 100 mummies was obviously too low and there was a large number of textiles, khipus, pottery, wooden artifacts, feather ornaments and bones. On-site emergency conservation, inventory and evaluation would not be possible in the time we had allotted.

In addition, the rainy season was upon us. The looters had exposed several mummies to the waterfall that often fell in sheets over the overhang and the mummies were rotting. Obviously, it was an important collection and in such critical condition that we could not leave it at the site with a mere report of what we had found. One archaeologist proposed enclosing the site with a wrought iron fence, but such a scheme was unfeasible. Following consultation with the head office of the INC in Lima, permission was granted to remove all of the material to Leymebamba. Roxie Walker, head of research at The Bioanthropology Foundation, helped secure funding for this move. We rented a house in Leymebamba and began hiring and training local people to help us receive and curate the materials. The staff of Centro Mallqui in Ilo came to Leymebamba to provide additional assistance and training.

Although we explored several alternatives, in the end the only realistic way to remove the mummies and offerings was using the horse trail. We used packing material to protect the artifacts. Eventually, we moved over 2,400 artifacts, including 219 mummies, much, much more than we had even expected. Despite the difficulties and hardships of the trail, nothing was damaged en route. Nevertheless, we were now confronting a much bigger undertaking than we had ever imagined.

Our first step was to train local people in the basics of conservation and collections management. Professional conservators offered basic training. Inge Schjellerup, a Danish archaeologist and expert on Chachapoyas, became a willing contributor, contacting us with Lena Bjerregaard, a textile conservator and weaver. Lena offered her expert guidance in confronting the enormous task of curating the large number of textiles. This volume presents her analyses of some of the most impressive and diagnostic textiles housed in the Museo Leymebamba.

The khipus featured among the most important components of the collection. Unfortunately, because the looters removed them from their original contexts, we will never know whom they accompanied; nonetheless, the Leymebamba khipus are the only extant collection of knotted string records from the cloud forest. Gary Urton of Harvard University is one of the leading experts in khipu studies. He secured funding for the conservation of the khipus, and his article in this volume presents a summary of his finds.

From the small network of mummy specialists, we invited anthropologist Horst Seidler, who heads the Austrian and Italian teams studying the Iceman found in the Alps in 1992. His visit to Leymebamba spurred his interest in the collection and he became intrigued by the concern of the local community to protect its heritage. Horst helped us define the need for a museum to house the collection and he was instrumental in obtaining Austrian financial support that contributed to the construction of the Museo Leymebamba. His participation has been instrumental in the design of the research program to study the mummies.

The museum's mummy collection is unique. The Inka-style clothing worn by many of the mummies indicates that they date to Inka times. The bodies had been eviscerated and treated, making them the first embalmed Inka mummies discovered in the cloud forest. The significance of this find is especially important, as zealous priests had destroyed most Inka mummies in Spanish colonial times.

Gerald Conlogue and Ron Beckett of Quinnipiac University registered the mummies by X-ray. They trained students and local people. The X-ray images showed that evisceration had not affected the thoracic cavity and that only the abdominal cavity had been emptied. Preserved lungs and other organs indicate great potential for future palaeopathology studies. A significant number of bodies suggest modifications indicative of tuberculosis. Differences in burial patterns between the Chachapoya and conquering Inkas also became apparent. The Chachapoya disposed of defleshed bodies in simple cotton bundles, while the Inkas wrapped embalmed bodies in several layers of cloth.

Creating a Museum

The Museo Leymebamba has had an enormous impact on the lives of local people. Formally, the museum belongs to the town of Leymebamba, although for the time being it is administered by Centro Mallqui – The Bioanthropology Foundation Peru. The goal is that the museum will eventually become self-sustainable, an objective that can only be reached with the support of tourism.

So far, the results have been positive: in 1996, before the discoveries at Laguna de los Cóndores, only a handful of tourists passed through Leymebamba, while in 2003, 8000 people visited the museum, 1200 of whom were foreigners. Most visitors, mainly students, are from Chachapoyas.

The museum blends in well with the immediate natural environment. Architects Rosanna Correa and Jorge

Ethnographic Hall, Museo Leymebamba. Photo: Adriana von Hagen.

Burga designed a building that uses elements of local architecture, while the surrounding gardens, planned by Liesel Stahr-Arrarte, highlight native flora. Peruvian museographer Rodolfo Vera contributed to the design of the exhibits. One especially innovative feature is the incorporation of the mummy storage room into the museum circuit. This reflects the museum's philosophy of integrating the public into the conservation of the collection, making visitors aware of the number of bodies and their conditions. In addition, the display incorporates the mummies into the life of the community, in much the same way as they did in the past when their descendants visited and cared for them.

The bulk of the financing came from Austria, the Bioanthropology Foundation and the von Hagen family. Leymebamba and neighboring towns contributed labor and materials. Of the $500,000 invested in construction and implementing the exhibitions, we spent close to half on wages and purchasing local construction materials.

The Museo Leymebamba has placed Leymebamba firmly in the northern tourism circuit, a route that includes the north coast sites of Sipán, Batán Grande and Túcume, as well as the famous Chachapoya settlement of Cuélap. Tourism is key to economic development in an area that has no other significant resources. Nevertheless, much remains to be done in integrating several other icons into the tourist circuit as well as improving infrastructure and access. Nevertheless, the museum fulfills one of our main goals: creating an icon for tourism, education and culture as well as instilling pride and a strong sense of connection with local communities, while at the same time serving as a fitting venue to house the extraordinary collection of materials from Laguna de los Cóndores.

The entrance hall of Museo Leymebamba is shaped like a traditional Chachapoya round house with thatched roof. Photo: Adriana von Hagen.

Lena Bjerregaard

Textiles, Materials and Technologies

In Inka society, as indeed throughout the ancient Andes, textiles ranked among the most valued objects, serving as ethnic and social markers. In provinces where the Inkas had consolidated their rule, local weavers incorporated aspects of the Inka style into their repertoire, creating both classic Inka-style garments as well as hybrid styles. Nonetheless, other areas continued to enjoy considerable autonomy, producing cloth much as they had before the Inka conquest. At the same time, the rulers of Tawantinsuyu, as the Inka called their realm, distrib-

Inka women wore a wrap-around dress and a shawl fastened with a metal pin. (Guaman Poma, *Nueva corónica* [1615], GKS 2232 4°, p. 225. Credit: The Royal Library, Copenhagen)

Inka men wore knee long tunics and shawls. (Guaman Poma, *Nueva corónica* [1615], GKS 2232 4°, p. 366. Credit: The Royal Library, Copenhagen)

uted standardized garments, especially tunics and the small bags used to carry coca leaves, among select subject peoples. Specialized weavers produced these garments at state-sponsored workshops in Cusco and provincial capitals. Stamped with the Inka approbation and symbolizing political power, these gifts were bestowed as rewards for loyalty or prowess in battle, as bribe or to seal diplomatic negotiations.

As a rule, ancient Peruvian weavers did not cut fabric. Rather, they produced cloth on the loom to the desired measurements with four selvedges and stitched the loom panels together to produce tunics, mantles, wrapped dresses, bags, etc. The Inkas rarely cut textiles and viewed such an act as profane (Stone Miller 1992:

22). It is therefore notable that at least three of the finest textiles housed in the Museo Leymebamba have been cut from the loom and stitched (e.g. CMA 2065, p. 71, CMA 845, p. 78, CMA 2082, p. 88).

By Inka times (Bosqued and Gómez 1980) geometric patterns and all-over designs had replaced the gods and mythical beings so widely used to decorate cloth in previous times. The most superb Inka tunics were woven in tapestry with camelid fiber wefts so tightly packed (up to about 120 wefts per centimeter) that ancient Andean cloth rivalled the finest weavings of Renaissance Europe. The two-ply camelid yarns of ancient Peru are some of the very finest hand spun fibers in the world (d'Harcourt 1975).

Drawings by the seventeenth-century Andean chronicler Felipe Guaman Poma de Ayala ([1615] 2001) as well as the account by the Jesuit chronicler Bernabé Cobo have revealed details of Inka attire. Men wore breechcloths, tunics that fell to the knees or below, mantles, headbands and carried coca leaves in small *chuspas*, or bags, while women wore long tunics or wrap-around dresses, pinned at the shoulders with *tupus*. Some dresses were sewn into a tube, and they were often cinched by a belt. Women also wore a folded mantle around the shoulders fastened by a *tipki* pin.

Many of the Leymebamba garments fall within the range of known measurements for Inka attire. A few of them are strictly Inka (e.g. CMA 2082, p. 88, CMA 671, p. 103, CMA 1795, p. 111, CMA 1836, p. 112), but the majority have Inka dimensions. These, however, are embellished with Chachapoya-style iconography (e.g. CMA 2069, p. 72, CMA 845, p. 79, CMA 676, p. 96, CMA 834, p. 100).

An Inka woman weaving on a backstrap loom. (Guaman Poma, *Nueva corónica* [1615], GKS 2232 4°, p. 217. Credit: The Royal Library, Copenhagen)

Fibers

Cotton

Native Peruvian cotton (*Gossypium barbadense*) is resistant and short staple (2.5–5cm) and grows naturally in at least five different colors: white, tan, light brown, dark brown and a greyish mauve. The hand-ginned fibers were spun with the spindle resting almost horizontally in a bowl. The spun threads were then plied, also on a spindle. Cotton thrives on the irrigated coastal plains, in temperate inter-montane valleys and in the tropical lowlands.

Camelids

The highlands, on the other hand, spawned the native Andean camelids – the domesticated llama and alpaca as well as the wild vicuña and guanaco. The camelids produce fibers that vary in luster, length and quality, ranging from the silky hair of the vicuña – the finest – to the coarse hair of the llama. Today, as no doubt in the past, alpacas supplied most of the fiber. The long, lustrous hair of the alpaca is about 15–20cm long and 10–75μm thick; averaging around 26μm (Paul 1979). Vicuñas, on the other hand, have shorter and finer hair (5–6cm long and 6–35μm thick). The Inka rounded up vicuñas, shearing them for their fiber. Each vicuña provides around 400gr of fiber (Majory 1986). The Inka reserved vicuña fiber for the finest textiles which only the Inka emperor could wear. Because the fibers of the llama are coarse, (10–150μm), they were not often used to produce clothing, but they did supply fiber for saddle bags, rope and wigs.

Camelid fiber takes dyes much more readily than cotton and, throughout the ancient Andes as in Chachapoyas, it was the fiber of choice for tapestry wefts and for embellishing plain-weave cotton textiles with embroidery and brocade.

Technology

Spindles

All Pre-Columbian textiles were produced from hand-spun yarns. Before the Spanish invasion, ancient Andean people spun some of the finest woollen yarns in the world. The uniformity, quality and spin/ply direction of camelid yarns (almost invariably Z-spun, S-ply, either two or three ply [A.P. Rowe 1997]) in Inka times hints at the existence of highland spinning centers that exported

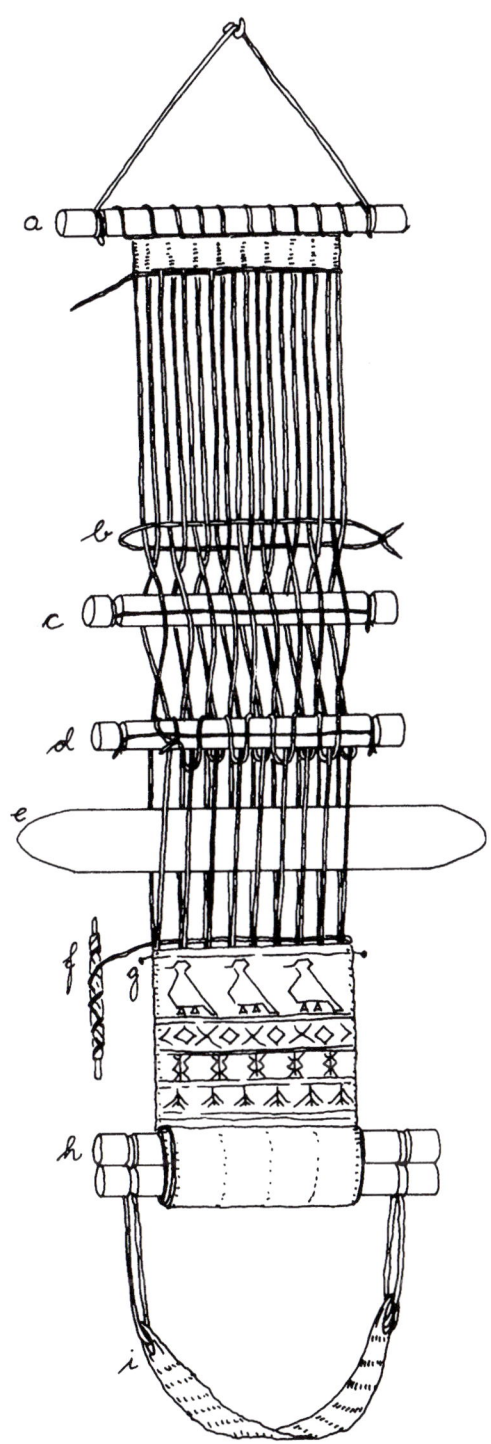

The backstrap loom. Drawing: Lena Bjerregaard.
a: Top beam. b: Cross-tie. c: Rod. d: Heddle. e: Batten.
f: Shuttle. g: Stretcher. h: Bottom beam.

yarn to the rest of the empire (d'Harcourt 1975) including, perhaps, Chachapoyas.

Occationally the cotton is Z-spun, but most of the cotton cloth in the Museo Leymebamba is made from single ply S-spun yarns, distinct from the camelid fiber yarns, which are all Z-spun, 2-ply S. The cotton yarns also vary in thickness and quality, suggesting that cotton was locally spun in pre-Columbian Chachapoyas, whereas camelid fiber yarns were manufactured under the aegis of the Inkas.

LOOMS

Before the Spanish invasion, ancient Peruvian weavers used horizontal and vertical looms. The Museo Leymebamba has examples of cloth woven on both loom types.

The horizontal loom consists of several loom bars; the top bar is attached by a cord to a fixed point, such as a post or a tree, and the bottom loom bar is fastened to a belt worn around the waist of the weaver; this is known as a backstrap loom. The fixed point is usually located higher up, so that the loom slopes down towards the weaver. Weavers are able to regulate the tension of the loom by bending forward or backward. The warp is attached to the top and bottom loom bars with a strong cotton cord that is removed after the weaving is completed, leaving selvedges at either end of the weaving. The last few centimeters of the warp are woven using thin needles so that the final product had four selvedges. Some of the Chachapoya textiles do not have four selvedges, but are cut along the top of the warp and secured at the top with a seam.

Backstrap looms allow long warps which can be rolled up on an extra bottom bar as the weaving progresses. The weaving, however, cannot be wider than ca. 75cm, as the weaver must control the entire width of the fabric by beating the weft down with a wooden weaving sword.

Looms can also be stretched horizontally and held in place by four stakes, as seen today in the southern Andes. This loom type has the same advantages and limitations as the back-strap loom.

The upright loom as used in Colonial Peru and earlier. (Guaman Poma, *Nueva corónica* [1615], GKS 2232 4°, p. 661. Credit: The Royal Library, Copenhagen)

The Inkas may have inherited the technology of the upright or vertical loom from the Wari (whose empire flourished ca. AD 600–1000). Wari weavers produced stunning tapestry tunics on looms consisting of four-sided frames, allowing more than one weaver to work on the piece simultaneously. In Inka times this kind of loom produced only the finest tapestry fashioned by select groups of skilled weavers.

Vertical looms could be set up in any desired width; Stone-Miller (1992) suggests that some looms could be folded after weaving the first half, allowing weavers to remain seated on the ground and weave all the way through the textile, although they may have stood to weave the second half. The tunics were woven from the side, so that the warp direction was horizontal when worn. Only weft-faced textiles with camelid fiber wefts were woven on vertical looms. Warps could be either cotton or camelid fiber. Two of the Leymebamba textiles (INCL III, p. 84, and CMA 2082, p. 88) are woven on this kind of loom. They both have cotton warps and camelid fiber wefts. All the other textiles at the Museo Leymebamba analyzed so far are woven on backstrap looms.

The loom beams, shed sticks and especially the weaving swords were made of strong wood. Llama or deer bone picks were used for laying in the patterns. Embroidery or sewing needles were made of cactus or algarrobo thorns or of metal.

TECHNICAL ANALYSIS

Note to the Reader: the definitions in the following discussion are taken from Irene Emery's *The Primary Structures of Fabrics* (1966). The techniques are divided by number of thread elements, while weaving and post-weaving techniques are presented at random.

1. One element: simple looping, knotting
2. Two elements: cord wrapping, twining
3. One set of elements: braiding
4. Two sets of elements (weaving): balanced plain-weave (mainly 2/1 but 1/1 and 2/2 also occur), warp-faced plain-weave, discontinuous warp, tapestry, complementary warp weave, supplementary warp weave, brocade (single faced, two-faced, double faced) and tubular weave
5. Decoration of fabrics: tassels, tie dye, pigment and embroidery

ONE ELEMENT

Looping is a doubling of a cord or thread back on itself so as to leave an opening between the parts through which another cord or thread may pass (Engelstad 1985).

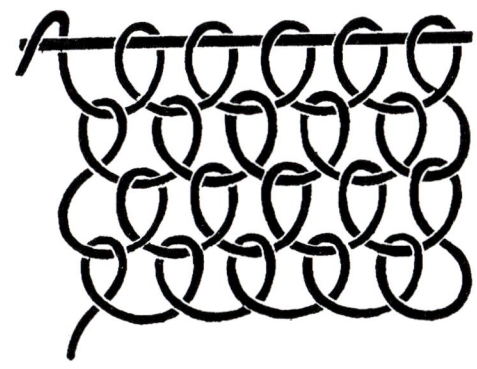

Looping. From d'Harcourt 1975.

Simple looping

Simple looping is created by what is known as the buttonhole stitch in sewing and lace-making, and as a half-stitch in rope work. Depending on whether the looping is loose or tight the fabric created can have an open net-structure or a crochet-like compact feel.

All the plant fiber bags in the Museo Leymebamba are made by simple looping, in which the yarn twists around the side of the mesh it has just formed.

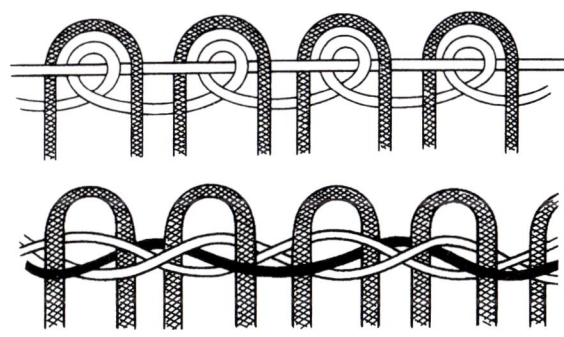

Camelid fiber fringes secured by cotton yarns – to be wrapped around a cord to produce furred cords. Drawing: Ulrich Gebauer.

Furred cords

Narrow fringes were made by twining two or three cotton strings through loops of camelid fiber, thus securing the loops. These were then cut open and tightly wrapped around or stitched to a core to produce a furred surface.

There are two headbands in the Museo Leymebamba

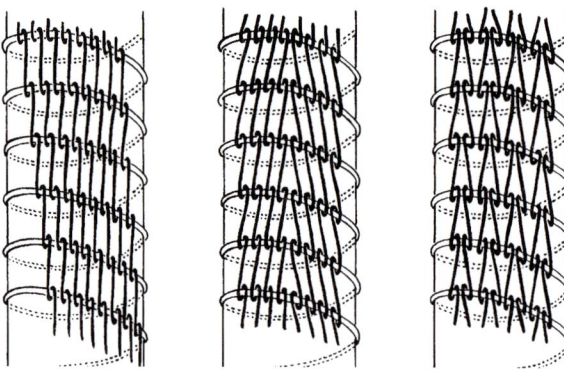

Cord wrapping with stem stitch embroidery. From d'Harcourt 1975.

(INCL 97, p. 95 and CMA 1834, p. 97) created in this technique.

TWO ELEMENTS

Cord wrapping with soumak embroidery

In this technique a number of cotton yarns serve as the core. Threads are wound in a spiral around the core and these spiralling yarns are then joined together by stem-stitch embroidery. This technique in seen in the tops of tassels and in the ornamental borders of certain garments and bags. The *tupu* cord (CMA 1795, p. 111) in the Museo Leymebamba is made using this technique.

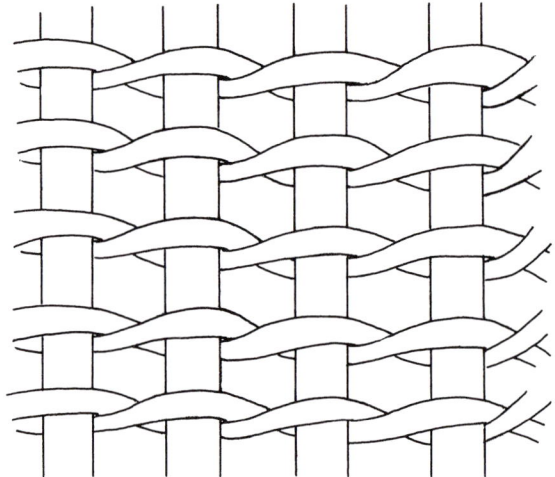

Half weaving. Drawing: Ulrich Gebauer.

Twining

The mat (CMA 1836, p. 112) is made in this half weaving technique. Flat, cut reeds have been joined together with camelid fiber yarns that intertwine regularly with a color pattern to create a stiff, flat "fabric" in which the reeds are completely hidden by the camelid fiber yarns.

ONE SET OF ELEMENTS

Braiding

Braiding is oblique interlacing where a set of yarns, tied at the top and loose at the bottom, are interlocked by passing over and under each other, changing in direction only at the edges of the fabric, where the elements turn back on the opposite diagonal. As many yarns as needed can be intertwined in this way. Examples of braiding in the Museo Leymebamba include simple braids composed of four to five plaits, forming parts of a net (INCL 96, p. 109) and a sling (CMA 839, p. 110).

Braiding. From d'Harcourt 1975.

Two sets of elements

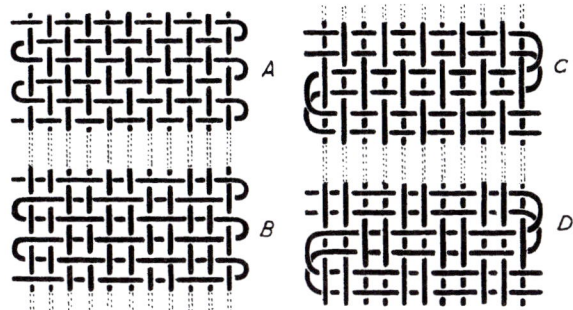

Plain weave. From d'Harcourt 1975.

Plain-weave

Plain-weave is the simple interlacing of warp threads stretched between two loom bars and a weft interlocked from side to side. Each weft unit passes alternately over and under successive warp units, and each reverses the procedure of the one before it, i.e. the warps are separated into only two groups, and all warps that lie above one passage of weft lie below the next and so on. Plain-weave can be varied by spacing the warps and weft differently or by grouping the elements into units, but basically the obverse and the reverse of plain-weave are structurally identical.

Some of the most frequently used plain-weaves in ancient Peruvian textiles comprise:

Balanced plain-weave (where the warp and the weft counts are completely or almost identical).

Unbalanced plain-weave, where warp and weft counts differentiate, i.e.: warp-faced plain-weave, where the warps completely cover the wefts (CMA 2069, p. 72, CMA 671, p. 102) or weft-faced plain-weave, where the wefts completely cover the warps, i.e. all tapestries (CMA 2082, p. 88).

Plain-weave with paired warps (CMA 600, p. 91) or paired wefts or both (CMA 569, p. 87). The majority of cotton textiles in the Museo Leymebamba collection have paired warps.

Discontinuous warp

This technique may be the most interesting of the ancient Peruvian weaving structures. It was probably never

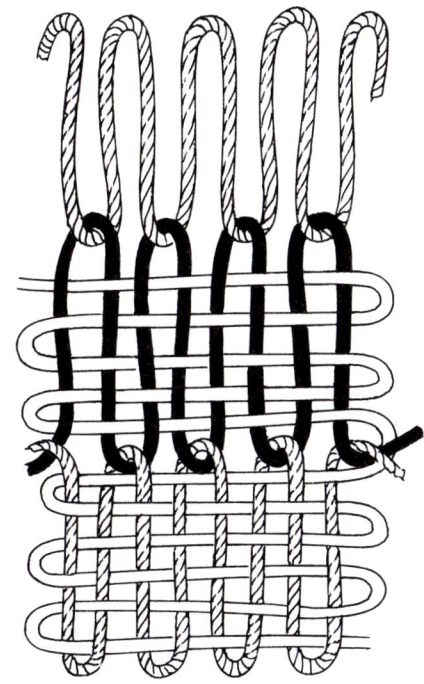

Discontinuous warp. Drawing: Ulrich Gebauer.

used extensively, if at all, outside of the Andes. It involves a special system of warp construction on which various weaving techniques can be used.

According to a desired pattern the construction consists of various warp segments of different colors, so that the warps, and sometimes also the wefts, turn back at the areas of color change. To set up an interrupted warp in this fashion, additional scaffold threads or rods are secured horizontally over the warp, and the warp threads reverse around these in the set up. Sometimes the scaffold threads are left in the finished fabric, at other times the warps are interlocked with each other, or the scaffold threads are removed after the weaving is finished and the warps are either held together with a common weft or are sewn together.

The discontinuous warp technique is seen in some of the plain-weave tunics at the Museo Leymebamba (CMA 2062, p. 69, CMA 2070, p. 75, CMA 2073, p. 76 and CMA 394, p. 83). There are no textiles with both discontinuous warp and weft in the Museo Leymebamba.

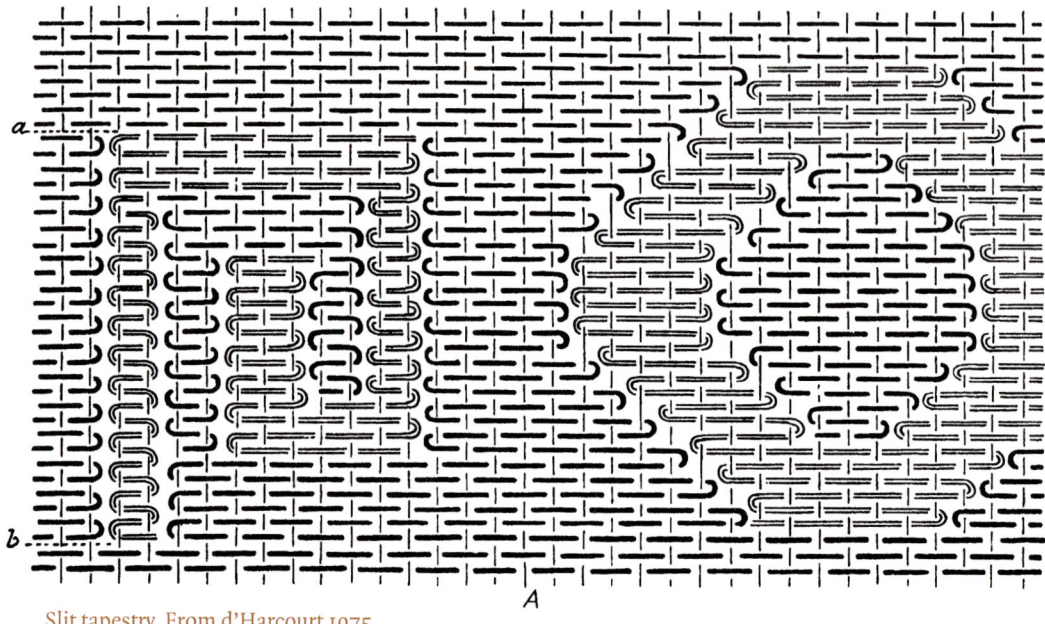

Slit tapestry. From d'Harcourt 1975.

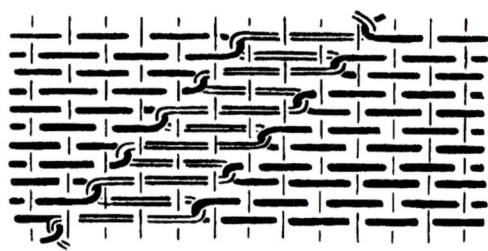

Interlocked tapestry. From d'Harcourt 1975.

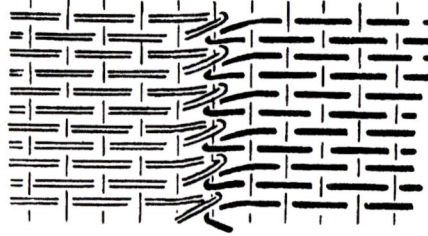

Dovetailed tapestry. From d'Harcourt 1975.

Tapestry

Tapestry is the name given to a mosaic-like patterning with discontinuous wefts in a weft-faced weave. Generally, tapestry involves two fundamental principles: hiding the warp with closely packed wefts to assure solid areas of color, and independently weaving wefts back and forth in their own pattern areas. The wefts are interlocked only partly across the warp and others are successively substituted to fill out the row, and in this way the wefts create solid color areas. The joins between wefts can be dovetailed, interlocked or slit.

In dovetailed tapestry the two wefts that meet turn around the same warp, while in interlocked tapestry the two wefts are looped into each other between the warps. Both dovetailing and interlocking can be done in many different ways, i.e. with each weft, every second weft or in pairs, or just occasionally.

In slit tapestry the wefts of adjoining color areas turn around neighboring warps, thus creating a gap along the vertical pattern lines. These slits can either be left open or sewn shut after the weaving is completed. Sometimes they are secured every one or two centimeters by a single interlocked weft.

The two faces of tapestry are identical in both structure and color patterning. All weft ends are concealed in the warp, and no loose ends are left hanging on either side of the weaving. (INCL III: dovetailed, p. 84; CMA 834: interlocked, p. 100; CMA 845: slit, interlocked and dovetailed, p. 79).

Single face brocade. Drawing: Lena Bjerregaard.

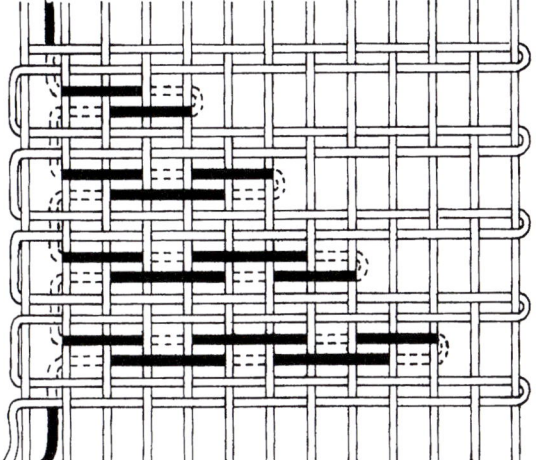

Two face brocade. From H. Engelstad 1985.

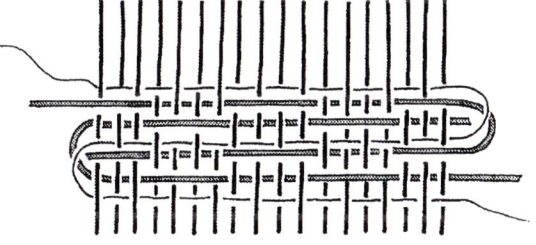

Double face brocade. Drawing: Lena Bjerregaard.

Supplementary weft weaving (brocade)

Brocade consists of supplementary weft threads that float over a ground cloth. This technique is often confused with embroidery. Chachapoya weavers favored this technique and examples abound in the Museo Leymebamba. For example:

Discontinuous wefts:
single-faced (CMA 2070, p. 75)
two-faced (CMA 845, p. 79, CMA 2073, p. 76)
double-faced (CMA 845, p. 79)
Continuous wefts (*lancé*)
single-faced (CMA 425, p. 95)
two-faced
double-faced

As in tapestry, the weft-ends of brocade are never left dangling but are always secured between the two warp layers.

In single-faced, discontinuous weft brocade, the pattern wefts are laid in between the two warp layers and pulled forward on the front side of the weaving, covering a varied number of warp threads. During weaving, the pattern wefts are always visible on the front side of the weaving. The pattern wefts never appear on the reverse side.

In two-faced, discontinuous weft brocade, the pattern wefts are worked through both warp layers. The warp threads covered by the pattern wefts on the front are uncovered on the back and vice versa, and so a negative pattern shows up on the reverse side of the weaving. During weaving, the pattern wefts are always kept on the reverse side of the weaving.

In double-faced, discontinuous weft brocade, the pattern weft is worked through both warp layers as in two-faced brocade. But in this case it is always worked over and under the same number of warp threads (normally four or six at a time). Without changing the shed the pattern weft is then worked back through the warp in the same way, this time going over all the warp groups it went under during the first pass. In this way the warp threads are covered on both sides with the pattern weft. Only after the pattern weft has been woven back and forth are the sheds changed and the ground weft woven.

The *lancé* brocading variations are the same as those mentioned above. The difference is that the pattern weft, instead of being discontinuous and partial, floats unbroken from selvedge to selvedge; partly between and partly over the two warp layers.

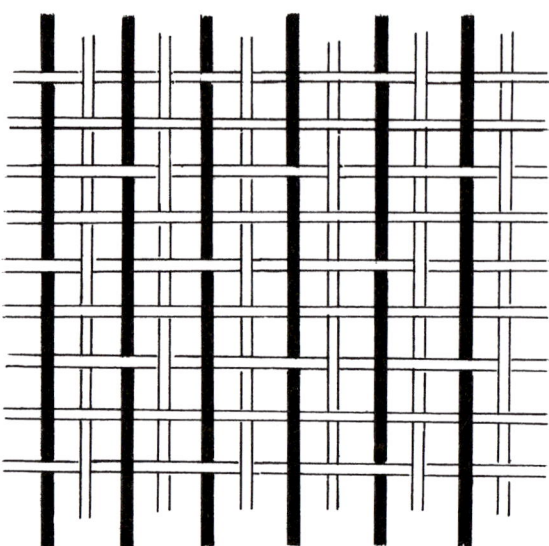

Complementary warp. Drawing: Ulrich Gebauer.

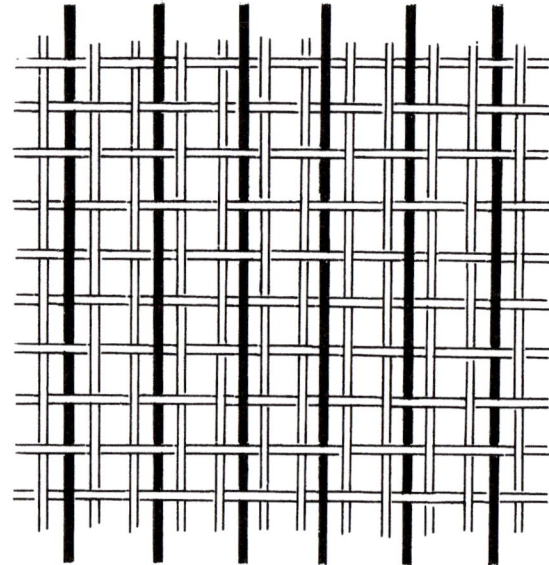

Supplementary warp. Drawing: Ulrich Gebauer.

Supplementary warp
Supplementary warp weave is a warp-faced, plain-weave with extra warps inserted in parts of the weaving. The extra warps are a different color from the basic warp and follow the basic warp shed but are left floating in places (normally over three wefts) on the two sides of the weaving (e.g. CMA 2069, p. 72 and CMA 2070, p. 75). These extra warps are often discontinuous, so the floating warp patterns are found only in limited areas of the weaving. This technique is very prominent in the Leymebamba textiles and is still used today by local weavers.

Complementary warp
Complementary warp weave has two warp systems of alternating colors, arranged so that the same warp pattern appears on the two sides of the weaving in alternating colors. The different warp yarns are never discontinuous, but always follow the complete warp (e.g. CMA 671, p. 103, CMA 397, p. 93).

Tubular weave
In this technique, the warp is woven in a cylinder created by a spiralling weft. The warps can be arranged in different techniques in a tubular weave – mainly plain-weave or complementary weave. In the Museo Leymebamba, tubular weaving is seen in bag straps (CMA 671, p. 103, CMA 768, p. 99).

DECORATION OF FABRICS
Embroidery
Accessory stitches used to decorate a textile. These include:

Running stitch
Running stitch is the simplest form of flat stitch in which the thread is carried forward in and out of the fabric to form a line of stitches on each face. In ancient Peru these stitches were used to stitch together most fabrics, and sometimes they are also used as a purely decorative element (e.g. CMA 2070, p. 75).

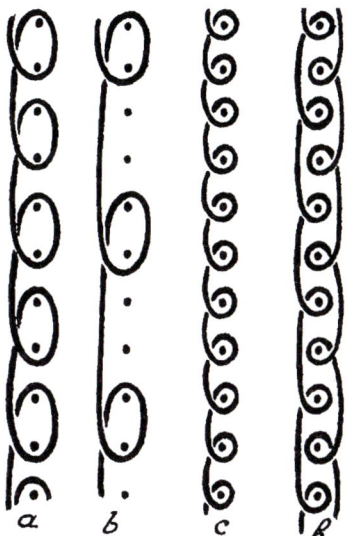

Stem stitch embroidery. Drawing: Lena Bjerregaard.

Tie dye. Drawing: Lena Bjerregaard.

Stem-stitch

Stem stitch is a flat back stitch, which goes over twice as many or more foundation cloth threads as it goes under in a circular movement. In the Museo Leymebamba it is seen in the embroidery used on the outermost layer of mummy bundles (e.g. CMA 2082, p. 88), and as the embroidery stitch on the wrapped-cord technique (CMA 1795, p. 111).

Chain-stitch

Chachapoya weavers used a chain stitch for embroidering the zigzag lines and the stylized faces on the outside of the mummy bundles (e.g. CMA 2073, p. 76).

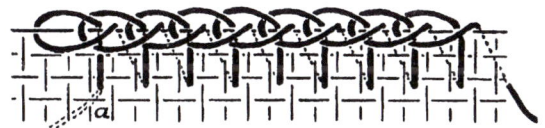

Loop stitch for edging textiles. From d'Harcourt 1975.

Loop-stitch

Loop-stitch, which is very similar to chain stitch, was often used for edging textiles (CMA 2082, p. 88, INCL 111, p. 84).

Tie-dye

Tie-dye (*planghi*) is a resist dyeing technique. The woven fabric (usually a light, plain woven fabric) is gathered at intervals in small, tightly-bound tufts. The entire fabric is then dyed, and the bindings are removed after dyeing. The resulting pattern consists of light circles – the color of the fabric before dyeing – (e.g. CMA 600, p. 91) on a darker ground.

Paint

In this decorative technique, pigments are fixed to a plain-woven textile. The pigment adheres only to the surface of the cloth and does not saturate the fibers. These pigments, probably mineral pigments applied as a thick paste, range from light to dark brown, and occasionally slate gray (e.g. CMA 756, p. 80, CMA 569, p. 86-87). The paint was applied with a brush made of camelid fiber, human hair or plant material.

Dye Sources

Some of the dyes employed in the Museo Leymebamba textiles were analyzed by Archim Unger of the Ratgen Forschungslabor in Berlin by means of HPLC (high-performance liquid chromatography). The results are published here with kind permission of Mr. Unger.

Fiber	Thread color	Dye stuff	Source
Cotton	orange	tanning agents	Walnut (*Juglans neotropica*)
Cotton	orange-red	Carajurin and derivates	Chicared (*Arrabidaea chica*)
Cotton	red-brown	Pseudopurpurin, Purpurin	Relbum root (*Relbunium ciliatum*)
Cotton	blue-green	Indigo	American indigo (*Indigofera sufruticosa*)
Cotton	blue	Indigo	—
Camelid	yellow	tanning agents	Alder (*Alnus jorulensis*)
Camelid	light brown	—	(*Juglans neotropica*)
Camelid	red	carminic acid	American cochineal (*Dactylopius coccos*)
Camelid	dark purple	Indigo	(*Indigofera suffruticosa*)

The presence of chicared, *Arrabidaea chica*, in the Museo Leymebamba textiles is especially interesting because at the time the analysis was made (2002) it was the first documented occurrence of this dye source in archaeological textiles from Peru. This member of the *Bignonia* family is a jungle vine used by the Orinoco Indians as body paint and to dye textiles. The leaves are an excellent dye source and in early Colonial times the leaves were exported from Venezuela to Europe. It produces a deep orange-brown. Among tropical forest people in Peru it is also used as a dye and an infusion from its leaves is employed to blacken the teeth.

Weavers in Leymebamba say that they use walnut (*nogal*; *Juglans neotropica*) to produce both a brown and a yellow dye. According to the analysis conducted by Archim Unger at the Ratgen Forschungslabor in Berlin, the bark collected from the two different trees that supposedly produced these two different hues contained the same chemicals in the same proportions. The two different colors may have been obtained by using different mordants.

Adriana von Hagen

Stylistic Influences and Imagery in the Museo Leymebamba Textiles

Introduction

The Chachapoya art style provides a fascinating window on a poorly understood culture known mainly for its fierce resistance to the Inka conquest. We are just beginning to unravel the origins and evolution of this little-known art style, thanks largely to the well-preserved burial offerings from Laguna de los Cóndores displayed in the Museo Leymebamba. The objects are playing a vital part in finding answers to the genesis of the style, revealing new imagery on perishable artifacts such as textiles and gourds.

Based on the little evidence that we have, "classic"

Cliff tombs at Diablo Wasi. Photo: Adriana von Hagen.

Chachapoya civilization – with its hallmark cliff tombs and circular constructions often embellished with decorative friezes – appears to have coalesced around AD 800. At various times in Andean prehistory the Chachapoya interacted with cultures living to the west of the Marañón – as seen, for example, in pottery influenced by the Cajamarca tradition – while at other times they seem to have flourished in relative isolation. Although the Chachapoya played a part in the greater Andean cultural sphere, their art and architecture convey a bold, independent spirit that sets them apart from their neighbors. Given Chachapoyas' location and apparent sporadic contacts, it is no surprise that its weavers produced cloth that assembled odd mixtures of technical and stylistic features drawn from many cultures and periods.

Even though the farm hands who discovered the Laguna de los Cóndores burial site in late 1996 churned through the tombs, slashing mummy bundles with

The Chachapoya site of San Antonio in the province of Luya, near Leymebamba. Photo: Adriana von Hagen.

Tree fern, Laguna de los Cóndores. Photo: Adriana von Hagen.

machetes and destroying valuable contextual information, archaeologists recovered more than 200 mummy bundles and a wide array of burial offerings dating to Chachapoya (ca. AD 800–1470), Chachapoya-Inka (ca. 1470–1532) and early colonial (ca. 1532–1570) times (Guillén n.d.a [1998], von Hagen 2000, 2002a, 2002b, 2002c, von Hagen and Guillén 1998, Muscutt 1998, Lerche 1998, 1999, Urton 2001, 2003).

Several lines of evidence support our search for the origins of the imagery and the stylistic as well as technical features of the textiles displayed in the Museo Leymebamba. These include iconography, weaving techniques (including spin and ply directions of the fibers), colors and dye sources, loom types and dimensions of the garments. In general, the imagery displayed on the Museo Leymebamba textiles is not Inka. It does, however, link to iconography found on other objects, especially pyro-engraved gourds, bamboo containers and pictographs at Laguna de los Cóndores and on a few other items, particularly a carved wooden lintel from the Chilchos valley north of Laguna de los Cóndores. In turn, some aspects of the imagery and several stylistic and technical features of the textiles have parallels with styles as early as Recuay, which flourished in the Callejón de Huaylas from around AD 200–500, and as late as Wari, whose presence has been documented in the Cajamarca area.

At the same time, some technical features of the Museo Leymebamba textiles match those of cloth analyzed from other Chachapoya and Chachapoya-Inka sites. At Los Pinchudos, for instance, Fernández (2002) identified two styles, local and Inka-influenced. The local style, mainly cotton, included S-spun fibers, warp

The tombs at LC1, Laguna de los Cóndores. Photo: Adriana von Hagen.

stripes and paired warps and wefts, common features of the Museo Leymebamba textiles. Inka-influenced textiles from Los Pinchudos, on the other hand, included weft and warp-faced textiles and 2 ply S camelid fiber. Cotton cloth shrouding a mummy looted from La Petaca featured paired warps and stripes of reddish brown, light blue and dark blue decorated with a stepped design of supplementary floating warps (Schjellerup 1997), traits also seen in certain Museo Leymebamba textiles.

While the images displayed on the Laguna de los Cóndores textiles and gourds are in many ways new, they also contain familiar Andean themes, artistic conventions and traditions. These include front-facing figures with splayed arms and legs, the heads or bodies of felines or hybrid animals shown in profile, baring prominent, interlocking canines, as well as hybrid creatures that combine the fearsome qualities of several animals, notably felines, caimans, raptors or serpents. The Chachapoya also employed artistic canons such as bilateral symmetry and anatropic organization (Kubler 1975); that is, an artistic convention that reveals a new facet of an image when it is viewed upside-down or sideways (cf. Burger 1992).

Many of these themes and conventions first appear in Cupisnique art, whose culture flourished on Peru's north coast ca. 1500–600 BC, and among coeval societies located in the upper Jequetepeque drainage, especially at the site of Kuntur Wasi (Onuki 1997). During the Chavín horizon (ca. 400–200 BC), a widespread religious cult stimulated works of art in metal, cloth, stone and ceramics across a wide swath of the central Andes. Several of these traditions and conventions recurred in various media over the next several hundred years in the art of Moche and of its highland contemporary, Recuay (ca. 200 BC–AD 700), as well as Wari (ca. AD 700–1000).

Working backwards in time, let us explore the various influences observed in the Museo Leymebamba textiles. These range from more obvious Inka imports and locally produced examples with Inka stylistic attributes as well as imagery on textiles displaying more subtle influences that may point to earlier links with Recuay and Wari.

INKA INFLUENCE

The Inkas in Chachapoyas not only made an impact on local religion and language, but they also transformed the region politically, imposing strict control over the rebellious Chachapoya and reshuffling the power of the local lords, *kurakas*. Moreover, the Inka dispatched the Chachapoya as *mitmaq* – colonists – to other parts of the empire. By some estimates (Espinoza 1967, Lerche 1995), the Inka shipped out as much as 50 percent of the population, while others were simply killed. In turn, the Inka resettled Chachapoyas with bureaucrats from Cusco, colonists from other parts of the realm, as well as with people loyal to the Inka whose mere presence foiled local foment.

Skilled Inka artisans, based either in Cusco or provincial centers, included three categories of state weavers who fashioned fine, usually tapestry-woven cloth, or *qompi* (A.P. Rowe 1978, J.H. Rowe 1979): *mamakuna*, or "chosen women", who wove fine cloth for the cult, sacrifice and for the Inka; wives of provincial administrators and *qompikamayuq*, male weavers. Garcilaso noted that *qompi* was not woven everywhere but "in provinces where the natives were most ingenious and expert in its manufacture ..." ([1609] 1966: 251). Cieza's observation that Chachapoya weavers "made fine and highly prized clothing for the [Inka], and they still make excellent garments and tapestry so fine and handsome that it is greatly esteemed for its quality" ([1553] 1959: 99), suggests that Chachapoyas served as a source of fine cloth not only in Inka times but during the Colonial period as well.

Qompi could only be worn by Inka kings and nobles and those who had received it as a gift from the ruler. Since the empire produced such great amounts of *qompi*, fine cloth ranked among the most common gifts bestowed on loyal subjects (each of whom also received jewelry, a llama and a *chuspa*, or coca bag, filled with coca leaves. [J.H. Rowe 1979]). Coincidentally, archaeologists recovered several Inka-style *chuspas* among the Laguna de los Cóndores burial offerings. In the early 1530s, when the Inka emperor Atawalpa named Guaman and the lord of Çuta de la Jalca as *kurakas* of Chachapoyas, he gave them "shirts of silver [the finest *qompi*, adorned with silver] and other things and women" while lesser

Inka-style bag for carrying coca leaves. Photo: Adriana von Hagen.

lords received "shirts of qompi" as well as "other things and women" (Schjellerup 1997: 333). *Mitmaq* colonists, on the other hand, were offered gold or silver bracelets as well as woolen and feather garments (J.H. Rowe 1979). Provincial lords were presented with *keros* (ceremonial drinking cups) of gold, silver or wood as well as *qompi* cloth. Excavators also found paired sets of wooden *keros* and feathered headdresses at Laguna de los Cóndores. Thus, the evidence indicates that provincial lords and/or *mitmaq* figured among those buried at the lakeside *chullpas*.

The vibrant Chachapoya textile arts point to a long tradition of cloth making that endured into colonial times. Even as the Spaniards began consolidating their hold over Chachapoyas, textiles continued to be a favored gift. In the 1540s, a local lord named Guayamamulos sent "... a gift of feathers and some *mantas* ..." to the Spanish captain Alonso de Alvarado as a peace offering (Cieza 1998 [1553]: 426). In the late eighteenth century, Don Juan Pisarro Guaman, descendent of the famous *kuraka* Guaman, listed "three *qompi* shirts", several mantles and other fancy, Spanish-style attire among his prize possessions, which he bequeathed to a local priest (Schjellerup 1997: 340). So well-regarded were Chachapoya weavers that the Spanish colonial administration set up spinning and weaving workshops (*obrajes*) at Chiliquin, Chachapoyas, Chuquibamba and in the province of Luya and Chillao that produced bed spreads, sheets, shirts, stockings, breeches, and slippers (ibid.).

Despite their Chachapoya imagery, some of the textiles do match the criteria for *qompi*, especially the all-tapestry tunic, INCL III, tapestry bag, CMA 834 and tunic CMA 845, with its elaborate tapestry waistband. Chachapoya tunics tend to be longer than Inka ones (as long as 95cm, although widths range from 70cm to 96cm). Nonetheless, they exhibit a number of Inka features such as tapestry waistbands, embroidered zigzag side seams and loop stitch embroidery on the necks, armholes and bottom edges.

Tapestry waistbands are a salient feature of Inka tunics. The tapestry waistband embellishing tunic CMA 845 may have been salvaged (judging by the array of repairs), from an earlier tunic and incorporated into a tunic with Inka attributes. These include zigzag side seams and loop stitch embroidery. Conversely, some of the Museo Leymebamba tunics may have been manufactured in colonial times. The Ica valley of Peru's south coast, for instance, witnessed a resurgence of local styles following the fall of the Inka empire (Menzel 1959, 1976). Similarly, as Inka power waned in Chachapoyas, weavers may have revived local textile traditions, creating a new style dominated by Chachapoya imagery but retaining telltale Inka elements. Archaeologists found a small wooden crucifix, glazed pottery and glass trade beads, indicating that the *chullpas* at the Laguna de los Cóndores continued to be used into early Spanish colonial times. Radiocarbon assays of *khipus* recovered from the Laguna de los Cóndores revealed several late dates ranging from 1582 to 1622 (Urton 2001; and this volume, p. 67).

A pair of Inka-style *keros*, ceremonial wooden drinking cups, found at Laguna de los Condores. Photo: Adriana von Hagen.

THE TROPICAL FOREST

Given the proximity of the Chachapoya to lower cloud forest peoples such as the Hibito and the Cholón, whose lands, in turn, bordered on those of lowland forest groups, we should also explore tropical forest imagery and influences in the Museo Leymebamba textiles. The Hibito lived to the east of Gran Pajatén (Abiseo) while the Cholón occupied territories to the north of the Hibito and to the southeast of the Chilchos, a Chachapoya subgroup (cf. map in Espinoza 1967, Steward and Métraux 1948). Like other Chachapoya sites in the Huallaga watershed, the Laguna de los Cóndores may have served as a strategic way station or a center for encounters with peoples from the lower Amazon basin to exchange products and produce, part of a widespread exchange network that crisscrossed the region.

The Hibito and Cholón may have supplied Chachapoyas with tropical forest resources such as *coca, capsicum,* spanish peppers, honey, resin, beeswax, wood, dyestuffs, medicinal and hallucinogenic plants and herbs, animal pelts, live animals for pets and the feathers of tropical birds used to fashion feather cloth and plumed headgear.

The material culture of the Cholón and the Hibito was essentially a tropical forest one (Schjellerup 1997, Steward and Métraux 1948). Ethnographic references note that in the mid-seventeenth century, the Hibito, Cholón and Payanso (who lived along the right bank of the Huallaga between the Huayabamba and Chipurana rivers), gathered wild honey, wore painted cotton *cushmas* (tunics) and used ear and nose ornaments. They painted their faces with *achiote* and dabs of blue *huitoc* (*genipa*) (Izaguirre 1923, Steward and Métraux 1948).

One mummy bundle recovered from Laguna de los Cóndores is shrouded in cotton cloth (apparently a tunic) painted with an all-over design that recalls those seen on tropical forest ceramics and textiles. Indeed, some of the artifacts from the Laguna de los Cóndores are unmistakable tropical lowland imports. These include feathered headdresses and desiccated animals not native to the cloud forest. A remarkably well preserved feathered headdress, adorned with *Amazona*

Mummy bundle wrapped in painted cloth with design reminiscent of the lowland tropical forest. Photo: Adriana von Hagen.

spanish parrot feathers, has a cane framework reminiscent of contemporary lowland Amazon headdresses (cf. Braun 1995: 68). A recent survey indicates that the forest around the Laguna de los Cóndores, in fact, does not boast many of the birds – cotingas, cocks of the rock, macaws, tanagers, etc. – sought after in Precolumbian times (ProAvesPerú 2003). The identification of several feathers embellishing headdresses found at the Laguna de los Cóndores indicates that they belong to a mix of montane and lowland forest species, such as *Cairina moschata* (Muscovy Duck), native to wetlands, rivers and lakes east of the Andes; *Oxyura jamaicensis* (Andean Duck), found at Laguna de los Cóndores and neighboring Quintecocha; *Ara macao* (Scarlet Macaw), *Ara ararauna* (Blue and yellow Macaw), *Amazona farinosa* (Mealy Parrot) and *Amazona amazonica*, (Orange-winged Parrot) (Susanibar 2003). The macaws and parrots are all native to the lowland tropical forest.

The desiccated animals, tours de force of taxidermy, appear to have been used as carrying devices of some sort, since some of them have slits behind their necks and an attached carrying cord. Conversely, they may have functioned as headdresses. The most notable example appears to be a margay (*Felis wiedii*), so well preserved that even its whiskers are intact. Its tail, forelegs and hind legs were stuffed with unspun cotton, and it has a bird bone inserted through its nose. A smaller feline has been tentatively identified as a margay or an oncilla (*Felis tigrina*), and it was found with spindles inside its pouch. The Laguna de los Cóndores is located at 2700 meters, well above the range of the margay, which is found below 900 meters (Emmons 1990). The oncilla, however, does occur up to 3200 meters.

WARI IN CHACHAPOYAS?

Based in the Ayacucho basin in Peru's south-central highlands, Wari began expanding around AD 650. The Wari presence in Cajamarca is well-documented, and includes sites with Wari-style architecture and pottery (both pure Wari and local, Wari-influenced styles) (Reichlen and Reichlen 1949, Shady and Rosas 1977, Watanabe 2001). It is, however, elusive in Chachapoyas and consists of a few Wari-style sherds found at Cuélap (Ruiz 1972) and a single sherd from Cerro Campanario near Uchucmarca (K. Muscutt, pers. comm., 2002, cf. Watanabe 2001).

The evidence suggests that Wari presence and/or influence in Cajamarca spanned several centuries (Watanabe 2001) and does not appear to have disrupted the local ceramic sequence or sparked social upheaval, as occurred on Peru's north coast (Castillo 2000, Watanabe 2001). Indeed, the Wari presence in Cajamarca may reflect the establishment of colonists from the Ayacucho area to secure resources from neighboring regions, such as Chachapoyas. Like the Inka, the Wari may have viewed Chachapoyas as a source of tropical forest products and produce, which they obtained via Cajamarca intermediaries. Cajamarca floral cursive style ceram-

Feather headdress recovered from Laguna de los Cóndores. The feathers have been identified as *Amazona spanish parrot*. Photo: Adriana von Hagen.

ics (contemporary with the final phases of Wari influence in Cajamarca) have been identified in Chachapoyas. The occasional Wari sherd in Chachapoyas points to exchange rather than outright occupation.

Evidence for Wari influence in the Museo Leymebamba textiles, however, is somewhat more compelling. Tapestry, for instance, was the preeminent technique employed in Wari tunics. Only one tunic, INCL 111, however, is woven in all-over dovetailed tapestry, while a small bag, CMA 894, is woven in interlocked tapestry. Three tapestry styles – dovetailed, interlocked and slit- have been identified in the Museo Leymebamba collection. Wari and Inka weavers favored interlocking tapestry while coastal weavers preferred slit tapestry (Conklin 1996, A.P. Rowe 1996, 1997). Cut-pile headdresses and tapestry headbands were also manufactured during Wari times, and both occur at Laguna de los Cóndores (although both items are also documented from Inka times). Several Museo Leymebamba tunics (CMA 394, 2062, 2069, 2070, and 2073) are composed of two loom panels stitched up the center and along the sides, leaving openings for the arms and the head. This typical Wari tunic assembly style was not used by the Inkas for fine tunics, although Chimú tunics are assembled in this manner (Chimú tunics, though, are often sleeved and waist-length to display matching loincloths). The Laguna de los Cóndores tunics, however, are long and rectangular, while Wari tunics tend to be square.

Tunic INCL 111 is the only all-tapestry tunic in the Museo Leymebamba collection recovered thus far (future unwrapping of mummy bundles may reveal other examples). The tunic was not found at the Laguna de los Cóndores *chullpa* burial site of LC1 and is said to come from a looted burial site on cliffs situated to the north of the lake, known as LC2. Although the tunic is fragmented, enough remains to reconstruct its original, as-worn measurements: 75 x 96cm, narrower and longer than standard provincial Inka tunics. Like Wari and Inka tapestry tunics, it was woven sideways on an upright or vertical loom. While several technical features (tapestry, loom type, and remains of loop stitch embroidery on edges) suggest an Inka affiliation, these features may also have been common to provincial Wari tunics. At the same time, although the checkerboard effect of the tunic's alternating Chachapoya-style feline and human heads recalls some Inka tunics, (especially the famous all-tapestry tunic at Dumbarton Oaks, cf. A.P. Rowe and J.H. Rowe, 1996); the patterning is also reminiscent of that seen on Wari textiles. Generally, Wari motifs tend to be figurative or abstractions of recognizable elements while Inka designs are usually geometric.

Wari weavers produced textiles composed of separately woven and tie-dyed patches painstakingly reassembled to create stunning weavings (cf. Stone-Miller 1992). Laguna de los Cóndores revealed several fragments of a tie-dyed mantle or tunic and a plain-weave cotton bag, half of which is decorated with blue tie-dye. The fragmented tunic or mantle is composed of long plain-weave cotton strips in blue, beige, brown, black and orange decorated with tie-dyed circles. The strips are stitched together, a much simpler assembly method than the elaborate Wari "patchwork" textiles.

South of Laguna de los Cóndores, at Laguna Huayabamba, a recently excavated tomb yielded a fragment of plain weave, tie-dyed cotton. The site predates the Inka occupation and has been radiocarbon dated to AD 1000–1150; a floral cursive Cajamarca style bowl found in the tomb has been dated to the same time (K. Muscutt, pers. comm, 2001; Briceño and Muscutt 2004). This discovery indicates that tie-dye was employed in Chachapoyas at the end of the Middle Horizon. Interestingly, a private collection of Wari ceramics (said to have been found at the site of Miraflores near Otuzco, 8 km from Cajamarca) includes a vessel portraying a man wearing a tie-dyed tunic and a four-cornered hat (Watanabe 2001: fig. 4). Tie-dyed Wari tunics are regarded as high-status attire (Conklin 1996). Wari portrayed the emblems of its religion on portable objects such as textiles; perhaps Cajamarca intermediaries introduced these into Chachapoyas, where local weavers imitated the new techniques.

Finally, Wari weavers also produced stunning feather tunics. Although these were all found in coastal graves, the feathers came from tropical lowland forest birds such as macaws and parrots, and Chachapoyas may have been a source for some of the feathers, as it was in Inka times (von Hagen 2004).

Earlier Influences

Excavations in Río Abiseo National Park, located in the southern part of Chachapoyas, indicate that people began settling this part of the cloud forest at the onset of the Early Intermediate Period, around AD 200, reinforcing the notion that the Chachapoya cultural tradition evolved locally (Church 1994, 1999). Early pottery excavated in Manachaqui Cave, on the fringes of Río Abiseo National Park, points to links with peoples to the east and to the north as early as 1500 BC, and ceramics dating to 900–400 BC resemble the pottery of southern Ecuador (ibid.). Other compelling data also signal contacts with people to the west. Pottery found at Gran Pajatén, for instance, is akin to that of Huamachuco, the Callejón de Huaylas (the Recuay and white-on-red styles) and perhaps the Callejón de Conchucos during the Early Intermediate Period, AD 200–600.

At the same time, several scholars have pointed out similarities between the stone-working traditions of late Gran Pajatén and the Callejón de Huaylas during the Early Intermediate Period, AD 200–600. Recuay artisans excelled at stone sculpture, producing tenoned heads that recall their Chavín ancestry, as well as freestanding sculptures, generally of human figures. The similarity between the splayed stance of a figure gracing a Recuay stone relief (Grieder 1978: fig. 148) and Chachapoya human images is especially compelling as is the cross design on the torso (a motif also found in Chachapoya textiles and pictographs). It is also especially notable in the treatment of human and feline heads carved in stone and tenoned into the walls of structures. A tenoned head of a feline still projecting from a house wall at the site of Runashayana near Chuquibamba features prominent incisors and teeth that wrap half way around the head, in a style reminiscent of Recuay tenoned heads (Muscutt pers.comm. 2001, refers to the site as Gentíl; cf Schjellerup 1997). Because of poor preservation of organic remains in the Callejón de Huaylas, little is known of the Recuay weaving style, but the few surviving examples indicate that Recuay weavers fashioned elaborate tapestry cloth.

Schjellerup (1996) remarks on the uncanny resemblance of small stone sculptures (ranging from 11 to 28.5cm in height) found near Agua Santa, in the prov-

A Recuay-style tenoned head on display in the gardens of the Huaraz museum. Photo: Adriana von Hagen.

ince of Celendín, Cajamarca, to Recuay Aija-style sculpture. Although the Celendín examples are much smaller, their inverted, T-shaped noses (indicating that they are probably wearing nose ornaments), as well as the emphasis on facial features (with the rest of the body almost devoid of detail) recalls the Chachapoya style. A carved stone plaque also found in the area hints at its Recuay ancestry: it depicts a feline in high relief surrounded by ray-like appendages that end in snake heads (Schjellerup 1996). The composition – a central figure surrounded by rays- is classically Recuay. Schjellerup (ibid.) argues that the Agua Santa sculptures may represent crude imitations of the Recuay tradition, pointing to links with the northern Callejón de Huaylas.

Finally, in the Chota-Cutervo area of Cajamarca, W. Isbell (1997) notes that several *chullpas*, which he dates to AD 200–500, are decorated with low to mid-relief carvings reminiscent of the Moche, Vicús and Recuay styles. He also points out that the Marañón river valley and its eastern and western tributaries as well as the Callejón de Huaylas, which runs parallel to the Marañón, are all distinguished by "megalithic mortuary monuments" (Isbell 1997: 268). Some of these tombs boast as many as four stories and recall the multi-story *chullpa* at Salsipuedes in the Atuén river valley, Chachapoyas (Isbell 1997, Jakobsen et al. 1986–87, Schjellerup 1997).

Laguna de los Cóndores

Laguna de los Cóndores lies in the heart of territory once occupied by the Chilchos people, a group of *ayllus* that formed part of the Chachapoya ethnic group (Espinoza 1967; Lerche 1995; Schjellerup 1997; Urton 2001, 2003). The Chilchos inhabited the area east of Leymebamba and northeast of Bolívar, between the Huabayacu and Chilchos rivers, both tributaries of the Huayabamba that flows into the Huallaga.

Preliminary evidence suggests that the Inka removed the earlier Chachapoya burials they found at the Laguna de los Cóndores *chullpas* and relocated them in two other tombs, both of which are hastily built, later additions lacking plaster and paint and embellishments such as friezes or deer antlers. The Inka then re-used the more elaborate *chullpas* built by the Chachapoya as tombs for their people, a mix, as noted earlier, that probably in-

A tenoned head at the Chachapoya site of Runashayana (or Gentíl). The wrap-around teeth recall Recuay-style carving. Photo: Keith Muscutt.

cluded Cusco bureaucrats and *mitmaq* as well as local lords and their kin. One tomb, Chullpa 1, contained the skeletal remains of several hundred individuals (S. Guillén, personal communication, 2000). Chullpa 1 did not contain mummy bundles – the main target of the *huaqueros*, who hacked apart the bundles with machetes in their futile search for gold – and its roof was covered in part by the collapsed beams of a wooden balcony. Consequently, this burial structure escaped the plunder.

In contrast to the other *chullpas*, which contained flexed, embalmed bodies wrapped in several layers of cloth, the human remains from Chullpa 1 consist mainly of disarticulated skeletons and of a few burials placed in baskets. Indeed, the bones appear to have been tossed somewhat unceremoniously into Chullpa 1. In addition, the excavations revealed decorated and non-decorated hollow bamboo containers and an extraordinary pyro-engraved gourd whose imagery, we believe, reflects the religious cosmology of the Chachapoya before the Inka conquest.

Pyro-engraved gourd recovered from Laguna de los Cóndores. Photo: Adriana von Hagen.

Rollout drawing of pyro-engraved gourd. Drawing: Cecilia Núñez.

A   B   C

Myth and Transformation

The pyro-engraved gourd (decorated by incision and burning) is unique. About 17cm high and 14.5cm in diameter, it is decorated with a 6cm-high band arrayed with pyro-engraved figures that form a complex scene. The gourd appears to illustrate a narrative of some sort, perhaps a scene from a Chachapoya myth. The protagonists are represented by the half-human, half-animal beings, possibly shamans that featured in the local religious cosmology. It appears that they are transforming themselves into felines, or hybrid animals, their supernatural alter egos. While the meaning of the myth portrayed on the gourd eludes us, the protagonists hint at a rich and vibrant symbolic world.

The scene is composed of five main figures (labeled, from left to right, A–E): Figure A is an upside-down feline with a fanged mouth, clutching a smaller animal. Figure B, a goggle-eyed, anthropomorphic figure with splayed arms, wearing ear spools, follows it. The lower half of the anthropomorphic figure – apparent when it is turned upside down – seems to be some sort of feline, judging by the rounded ears, the fanged teeth and the zigzag markings on the tail-like appendages that emerge from its head to become either the arms or forelegs of the lower figure or the legs of the anthropomorphic figure above it. These zigzag markings also appear on the tails of the other felines.

Next in the sequence comes Figure C, a right-side-up feline with a fanged mouth whose tail is held in the left hand of the fourth figure, D, an anthropomorphic being sporting a double row of teeth. In its right hand, Figure D holds the tails of the last figure, E, a splayed feline or some sort of a hybrid animal, viewed from above as if it had been filleted like a fish. It has a wrap-around fanged mouth with impressive upper and lower canines and a double tail.

While Figure E's double tail may have some deeper significance, it can also be interpreted as a Chachapoya convention for portraying a subject with bilateral symmetry, since animals do not normally have two tails. In addition, it recalls the tail-like appendages emerging from the creature beneath Figure A. The tails are similar to those of a profile feline, 8.3cm high, pyro-engraved on a hollow bamboo container, also found in Chullpa 1. The tails on the bamboo container feline have zigzag markings like the ones on the gourd and it also has fanged teeth, a curlicue on its snout and a circle on its ankle.

The images on the gourd recall those found on a wooden lintel at a looted burial cave near the Chilchos valley (Lerche 1995). The 3.26m-long lintel had originally been placed over the cave entrance, which was also embellished by slashes of red paint. On either side of the lintel perch two carved human figures, one of whom

D   E

wears an *unku*-like garment and sports ear ornaments similar to those found at the Laguna de los Cóndores. The other human figure wears a headdress adorned with a horseshoe shaped ornament and he plays the panpipes.

The human figures flank an animal that Lerche describes as a caiman-feline hybrid. It has, however, only upper incisors and not the interlocking canines depicted on the gourd figures. The animal has swallowed the head of a smaller animal, lacking a tail, which Lerche says residents of the Chilchos valley identified as an *añuje*, or brown agouti (*Dasyprocta variegata*). The eyes, the rounded ears and the circles on the ankles and on the snout of the caiman-feline hybrid recall the splayed feline on the Laguna de los Cóndores gourd. The similarity between the Chilchos and Laguna de los Cóndores images suggest that they are local variations of wide-ranging Chachapoya religious and symbolic imagery.

Related Imagery

Similar imagery to that on the gourd and the bamboo container appears on some of the Museo Leymebamba textiles, such as, for instance, a tunic recovered from the mummy bundle of an adult male. He wore a bone nose ornament and his extended earlobes, which once held earspools, indicate that he was an *orejón*, a sign of status among many ancient Andean peoples, including the Inkas and the Chachapoya.

The body had been wrapped in five layers of textiles. The outer wrapping consisted of plain weave cotton, dyed blue, and decorated with a chain-stitch cotton yarn arrayed in a zigzag pattern around the bundle. Like many of the mummy bundles from LC1, a stylized, embroidered face and a braid emerging from the top of his head, topped the bundle. The next textile was plain, as was the fifth, while the third was a disassembled tunic (CMA 2069) composed of two panels, each 38cm wide and about 1.80m long. The two ends had been basted together and wrapped around the body.

The fourth textile was a tunic (CMA 2070) placed over

Hollow bamboo container found at Laguna de los Cóndores. The image portrays a profile feline with a double tail. Photo: Adriana von Hagen.

Detail of 3.26 meter-long wooden lintel discovered in a burial cave in the Chilchos valley, northeast of Laguna de los Cóndores. Photo: Adriana von Hagen.

the body with the neck slit sewn shut over the head. It is composed of two panels, each about 39cm wide and 1.90m long (97.5cm long and 79cm wide, as worn), sewn up the sides and the center, leaving openings for the arms and the neck. (The neck slit was subsequently sewn shut when the tunic was placed over the body in preparation for burial.) Below the neck slit, on either side of the tunic is a feline, 7.1cm high, with an arching tail embroidered in blue and red camelid fiber. The tunic's 5.5cm-wide fringed border bears volute-like designs in interlocking tapestry and profile feline heads in brocade. The brocaded figures on the shoulders depict seated profile felines, 3.6cm high and 7.3cm wide, with circles on their snouts and tails that end in feline faces similar to Figures A and C on the gourd from Chullpa 1.

Mummy bundle of an adult male during unwrapping. He wears a tunic, CMA 2070, see following page. Photo: Adriana von Hagen.

Tunic, CMA 2070. Photo: Adriana von Hagen.

Detail of shoulder, tunic CMA 2070, shows a row of seated, profile felines whose tails end in feline heads. Photo: Adriana von Hagen.

The central part of the tunic is divided into two sections, one of blue cotton with the remains of camelid fiber embroidery and another of brown cotton decorated with two pairs of woven figures, (in warp-faced plain weave with supplementary warp floats), each 13.2cm high and 12.3cm wide.

These sets of figures are mirror images of each other and have splayed arms and legs and diamond-shaped designs on their torsos. An upside-down view reveals a creature akin to Figure E, the splayed feline on the gourd. The tunic image has similar ears and wrap-around teeth with upper and lower incisors. The tunic image can also be read sideways, forming two profile felines. Profile felines appear in a number of guises on the Museo Leymebamba textiles. Some, like those embellishing tunics 2070 and 724 (as well as the gourd from Chullpa 1) have tails that end in feline heads. Many display fearsome fangs while others have teeth but no fangs.

The overall style and imagery of tunic 2070 are remarkably similar to a tunic said to have been found in either the Virú or Chicama valleys. Because the tunic be-

Detail of central panel, tunic CMA 2070. It portrays a splayed figure with a diamond-shaped design in its torso. Photo: Adriana von Hagen.

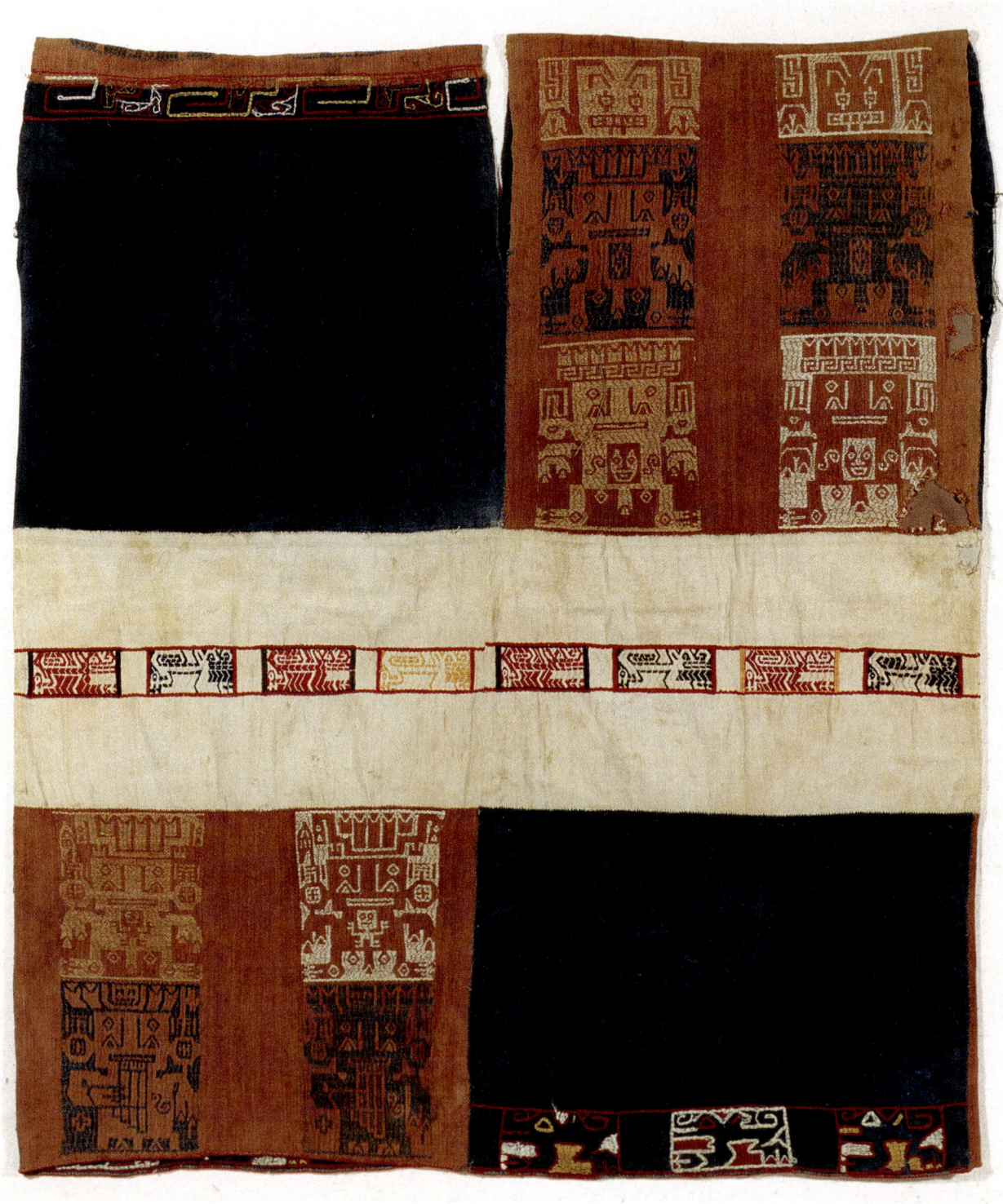

Chachapoya tunic in the Textile Museum in Washington. Mus. no. 1962.6.1. (Credit: The Textile Museum, Washington D.C.)

longed to an antiquities dealer who probably purchased it from a looter (who are notoriously vague about provenance), it may in fact come from Chachapoyas, despite its alleged coastal provenance. It too is composed of brown and blue squares, and fashioned of two panels sewn along the center and the sides. The waistband displays standing profile felines in brocade that are very similar to those on CMA 724 (although the tails of these felines end in small feline heads, recalling the ones on the gourd and the seated profile felines on the shoulders of CMA 2070).

The top left shoulder appears to be decorated with a geometric, embroidered design, while the lower right hand side of the tunic shows embroidered, seated profile felines. The upper right hand corner displays felines, whose limbs appear to emerge from the neck to encircle the face, recalling the feline on the tapestry fragment, CMA 676. Unlike CMA 2070, which has two sets of figures on one side of the tunic, the AMNH tunic is decorated with two pairs of human figures arrayed in the lower left and upper right hand corners. This section of the tunic is executed in the same technique as CMA 2070: warp-faced plain weave with supplementary warp floats.

The human figures are most extraordinary. All wear elaborate feathered headdresses and earspools while their torsos contain geometric designs, feline heads or human figures. All have circles on their ankles and display male genitalia (also seen in the splayed human figure on tapestry fragment CMA 676). One set of figures plays the panpipes. The treatment of the noses is quite similar to that of the brocaded human faces decorating the left hand edge of tunic CMA 2073 and of the splayed human figure on the tapestry waistband fragment, CMA 676. The flaring nostrils suggest that the human figures are either mustachioed or wear nose ornaments.

Finally, the mix of weaving techniques: warp-faced plain weave with supplementary warp floats, brocade, embroidery and the assembly style (two panels stitched up the sides and the middle) leave little doubt about the AMNH tunic's Chachapoya affiliation.

Related iconography is seen on a slit tapestry fragment (CMA 676) found discarded among the looted offer-

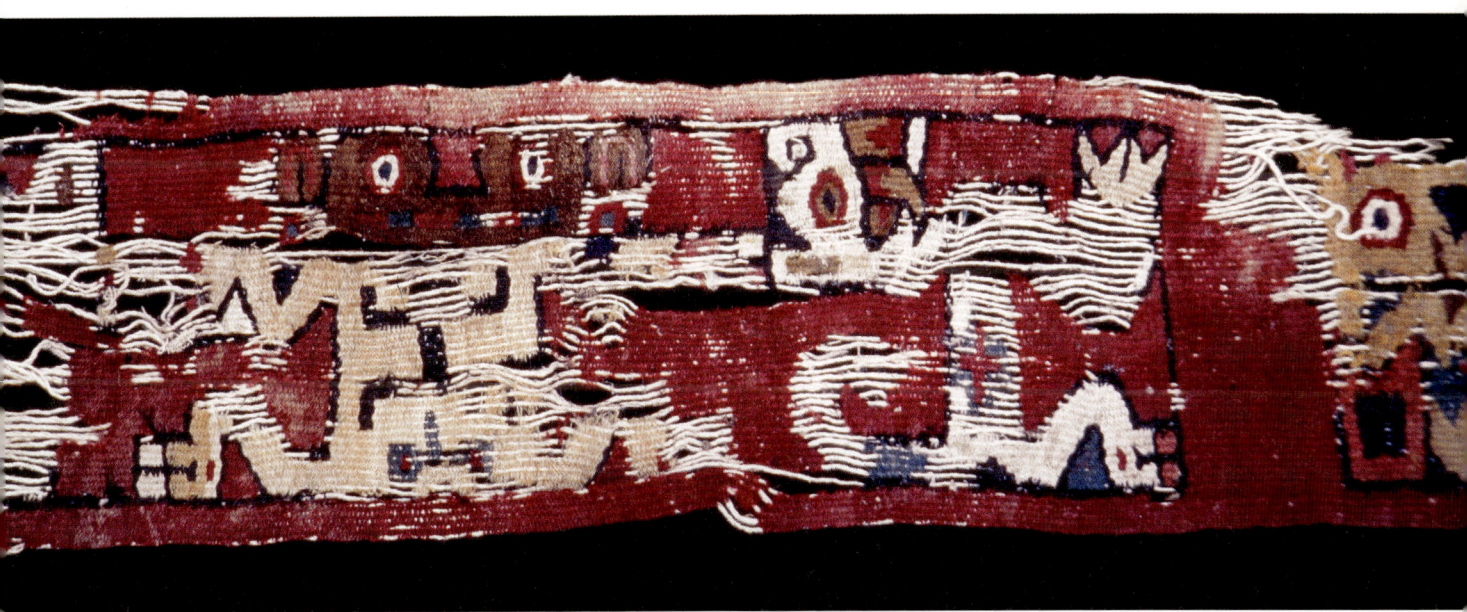

Detail, fragment of slit tapestry, CMA 676. Probably the waistband of a tunic, it features an anthropomorphic figure grasping the animal next to it. Photo: Adriana von Hagen.

ings at the Laguna de los Cóndores. It probably formed the waistband of a tunic and its composition echoes that of the gourd. Images include a 7cm-high anthropomorphic figure wearing ear ornaments, with splayed legs and arms, and grasping the animal next to it. The face of this fanged animal, with a circle on its snout, resembles those of the felines displayed on the gourd and on the bamboo container.

Finally, a Middle Horizon textile said to be from Nasca and today housed at Lima's Museo Nacional de Arqueología, Antropología e Historia, presents imagery almost identical to Figure E on the gourd. Woven in tapestry, it shows a splayed figure, apparently a feline, viewed from above, with similar pelage markings, circles on the ankles, and imposing crossed fangs.

Splayed images are a Chachapoya hallmark, found on textiles, in pictographs, on pyro-engraved bamboo containers, on carved stone and in stone mosaic friezes. A cotton and camelid fiber tapestry bag, or *chuspa*, in the Museo Leymebamba (CMA 834) portrays two splayed anthropomorphic images, in red, on a gold background. Feathered headdresses crown their heads and their inverted, T-shaped noses suggest that they are wearing nose ornaments.

The figures on the bag recall the stone mosaic frieze embellishing one of the structures at Gran Pajatén as well as a carved block of sandstone found in another building at Gran Pajatén (see illustrations in von Hagen 2002c: 132–137). Splayed anthropomorphic images also appear on a Museo Leymebamba painted tunic, CMA 756.

While some splayed images portrayed on the Museo Leymebamba textiles are recognizably human, the ones featured on tunics CMA 845 and 2065 are odd, hybrid creatures. CMA 845, for instance, depicts a series of five creatures on either side of the tunic (forming part of a continuous tapestry waistband). In typical Chachapoya fashion, their legs and arms are splayed and their torsos are embellished with geometric designs. Three of the figures on side A of the tunic portray the same diamond-shaped checkerboard designs on their torsos while the ones at either end display distinct patterns. The checkerboard torso designs echo the overall checkerboard effect of the tunic's alternating squares of brown and white cotton. Each of the figures is colored differently, ranging from white, pink and khaki to gold, and most have cirlicued ears, clothes peg noses and smiling mouths. The first figure (once colored white, most of which has disintegrated) differs from the others. Its hands reach as high as its head and it lacks the cirlicued ears of the others.

Each figure is bordered on either side by a dark line; at first glance, these appear to be staffs, but they are not being held. The figures on tunic CMA 2065 and groups of figures on tapestry fragment CMA 676 are similarly edged with dark lines, suggesting that this is an artistic convention (in the case of the tapestry waistband fragment they may be enclosing protagonists in a particular scene).

The iconography of tunic CMA 2065 is especially intriguing as is its patchwork assembly style (composed of 14 separate pieces). The waistband and bottom edge of the tunic are each arrayed with eight figures woven in tapestry. Like the creatures on CMA 845, not one figure is alike. Each one has a different geometric design woven into its torso and all the figures are bordered by a line; again, these do not appear to be staffs but serve, rather, to define the design unit. The creatures' bi-lobed heads are somewhat reminiscent of frogs. In fact, the creatures on CMA 845 with their smiling mouths are also somewhat froglike as are the heads of the more human figures on the gourd, although the creatures on the textiles lack the bulging eyes.

Since, as we have argued, the gourd may represent a scene from a Chachapoya myth, showing its protagonists transforming themselves into supernatural hybrid creatures, the figures on CMA 845 and 2065 may also refer to the same myth or to another tale of transformation. Frogs, of course, transform from fishlike tadpoles into

Tapestry weave, bag, depicting splayed figures, a Chachapoya hallmark. Photo: Adriana von Hagen.

Detail of waistband, tunic, CMA 845. Photo: Adriana von Hagen.

amphibians with human-like limbs, a phenomenon that may have intrigued the Chachapoya and imbued frogs with supernatural qualities.

In the 1960s, Gerald Taylor (1996) collected oral histories from Quechua speakers in the towns of Olto and Lamud in the province of Luya, Chachapoyas. In one, the Tale of the Town of Olto, a group of people searching for a place to settle undergoes a series of travails until they stumble on a lake filled with tadpoles. They found their town, Olto, on its shores (The ancient inhabitants were called Olcthug; Taylor notes the similarity between Olcthug and Quechua, *olto*, tadpole). While using oral histories, compiled 500 years after the Inka conquest of Chachapoyas and tainted by Christianity, to reconstruct ancient Chachapoya beliefs is speculative at best, it is nonetheless intriguing that tadpoles feature in tales that seem to suggest myths about founding ancestors and the origins of communities.

Conclusion

The iconography displayed in the Museo Leymebamba appears on objects manufactured relatively late in Andean prehistory. Yet, given the paucity of comparable examples from other parts of Chachapoyas, the pre-Inka Chachapoya imagery in the Museo Leymebamba collection appears as if from nowhere, with no documented antecedents. The discovery and excavation of similarly well-preserved tombs could help unravel the origins of Chachapoya cosmology and iconography. Even so, the mummy bundles, textiles and other burial offerings from Laguna de los Cóndores provide a first look at new aspects of the little-known Chachapoya art style and mark a beginning in the search for its origins.

Gary Urton

The Khipus from Laguna de los Cóndores

One of the most surprising and in many ways unexpected groups of artifacts encountered in what was already an extraordinary discovery of mummies and associated burial goods at Laguna de los Cóndores was a collection of 32 khipus (see p. 68). This discovery is especially important because the khipus from Laguna de los Cóndores are the only ones found in any context other than graves from the dry desert coast of Peru or northern Chile. Indeed, all of the other known samples in museum and private collections around the world – some 600 in all – came from the coastal desert.

The term khipu, which is from the Quechua word for "knot", refers to the knotted-string devices used for record keeping in the Inka empire. Khipus are composed of a main, or primary, cord – usually measuring about 0.5–1cm in diameter – to which is attached a variable number of more delicate strings, called pendant cords. The primary and pendants cords may be made of either cotton or camelid fiber. All but a few strings on the khipus from Laguna de los Cóndores are cotton. Pendant cords are often quite colorful, reflecting the different natural colors of the cotton or camelid fibers used to make the strings or the brilliant hues of dyed strings. Pendant cords are usually knotted in a system of knot placement that indicated values in the decimal place notation system used in Inka state record keeping. That is, knots

Khipu draped over rock at Laguna de los Condóres. Photo courtesy of Keith Muscutt.

UR6 - The Calendar khipu from Laguna de los Condóres. Photo: Gary Urton.

of the type called figure-8 knots (indicating ones) and those called long knots (indicating the units 2-9) were tied near the bottom of pendant strings. Single knots, indicating the full decimal values (e.g., 10s, 100s, 1000s, etc.) were tied on successively higher levels on strings. Thus, the placement of knots having decimal values was organized along strings on the same principle – but rotated 90° to the vertical – as the western European decimal place notation system

Because Chachapoyas fell under Inka control only about 50 years before the Spanish conquest of Peru, in 1532, it is intriguing to consider how and why *khipus*, the most esoteric of Inka recording devices, came to be interred, along with a large collection of late pre-Hispanic mummy bundles, in this far off and often rebellious corner of the empire. Given the rather poor state of our present knowledge of the late Chachapoya and Chachapoya-Inka occupation in the area of the lake, we cannot provide satisfactory answers to this question. In general, however, wherever the Inkas established themselves either by alliance or conquest in a given territory, they considered it vital to introduce the accoutrements of state administration. *Khipus* ranked chief among

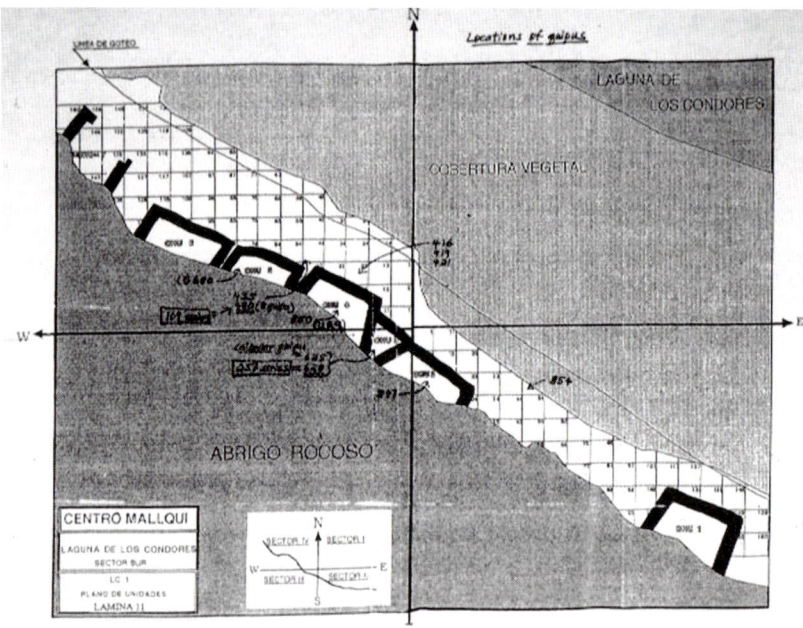

Top: UR22 – *Khipu* with cords attached to wooden bar. Photo: Gary Urton. Bottom: Locations of *khipu* finds at LC1.

these items, serving as instruments to record affairs of state such as census information, tribute records, and other accounts. Khipus allowed local, Inka-appointed officials to oversee the newly acquired territory for the benefit of the Inka.

According to the *huaqueros*, or grave robbers, who saw the *chullpas* (burial chambers) at Laguna de los Cóndores just prior to their ransacking, some of the khipus were draped across, or over, groups of mummy bundles. Like all of the other grave goods and mummy bundles, the khipus were thrown out of the tombs onto the ledge where the *chullpas* are located and then later were thrown back into the chambers before the salvage operation took place. As a result, the association of specific khipus with particular *chullpas* and mummies was lost forever. This information would have proved of inestimable value in helping us to understand the relationship among khipus, mummy bundles (with their associated textiles) and other grave goods.

What does seem to be clearly indicated from the grave goods, including the khipus, however, is that there were Inka officials, like the *khipukamayuq*, buried at the site of Laguna de los Cóndores. There may as well have been other classes of Inka subjects buried at the site, such as *mitimaq* colonists who were forced to move into the area from their distant home territories. Future analyses of the burial goods at the site may help to clarify the demographic composition and geographic origins of bodies mummified and buried in the Laguna de los Cóndores *chullpas*.

Nonetheless, a number of general observations can be made about individual khipus, as well as about two very interesting sets, or groups, of khipus that were tied together. As shown in the inventory of the Laguna de los Cóndores khipus provided in Appendix on p. 68, the majority of the khipus (i.e., 27 of 32 samples) were found at what is known as LC1, the *chullpa* burial site overlooking the lake. The remaining five khipus were found at a site known as LC2, another burial site located across the lake from LC1, on a steeply sloping hill high above the Siogue river. The khipus interred with the mummies at LC1 are today generally better preserved than those that were found in LC2. This differential preservation reflects more recent looting and salvage archaeology at LC1 while LC2 was looted several years previously and its khipus were more exposed to the elements.

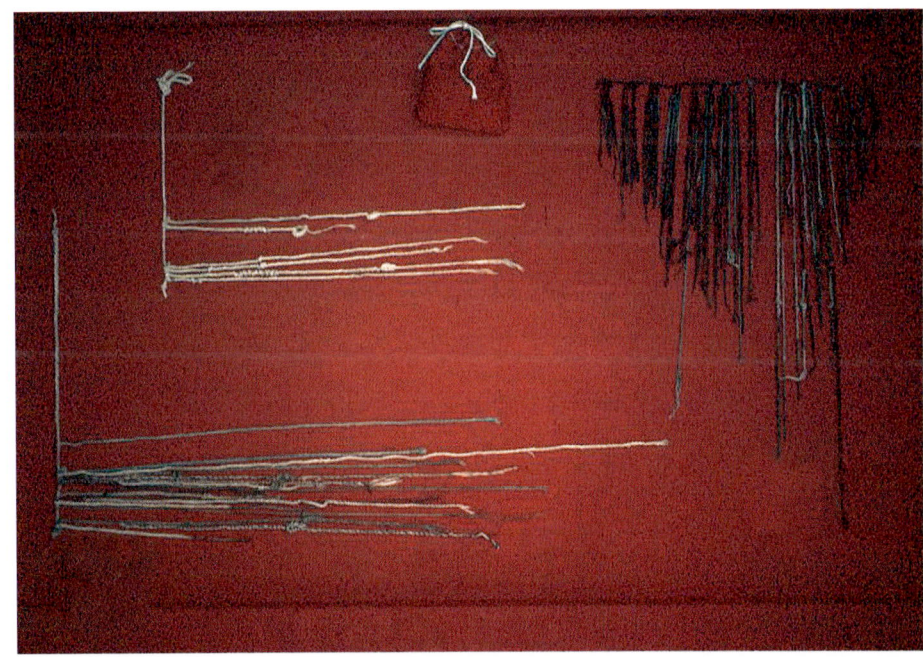

Three of the khipus composing the 109 series linked set. Photo: Gary Urton.

Ten of the khipus (including all five of those from LC2) were considered too fragile to manipulate. As a result, structural features such as spin, ply and knotting directionality could not be recorded. For this reason, only 22 of the 32 samples were studied and assigned "UR" numbers (numbers assigned to the khipus by the author).

The khipus range from ones with fewer than 20 pendant cords to others that contain more than 700–800 pendants. One very large khipu (p. 63), UR6, contains 754 pendant cords. In a recent article (Urton 2001), the author argued that this khipu represents a two-year calendar. This interpretation is based on the fact that 730 of the khipu's pendant cords are organized into 24 groups of 29, 30 or 31 strings. These groupings are interpreted as 24 lunar months comprising a two-year calendar of 12 lunar months each ($365 \times 2 = 730$).

One of the most remarkable and structurally complex samples is khipu UR22, whose primary cord passes through holes drilled in a wooden bar (p. 64). The 266 preserved pendant strings were attached to the primary cord along the long sides of the bar, as well as from the bottom of the bar, between the edges of the two long sides. This produced pendant strings organized in three planes suspended from the wooden bar. Unfortunately, this khipu, reportedly quite colorful at the time of its discovery, was washed with detergent soon after it came into the possession of the grave robbers. Consequently, the pendant strings are almost completely bleached white.

As mentioned earlier, several of the khipus were found tied together into linked groups, or "bundles". I refer to these two groups of khipus as the "109 series" and the "257 series", after their Museo Leymebamba accession numbers. Both of these linked groups of khipus were found inside, or immediately in front of the six chullpas at LC1. As noted, there was a considerable amount of mixing up of khipus, mummies, and other items in the burial chambers at the time of their discovery and plunder by the huaqueros. The khipus were recovered during salvage operations and excavations in the locations noted in p. 64, as reported in Sonia Guillén's salvage report (n.d.a)

The 109 series comprises seven khipus (109.1–6, with 109.2 composed of two small khipus) that were all tied together, as well as two additional khipus (109A and B) that were found close by, but not actually tied to, the other seven khipus (p. 65). Therefore, there is some doubt whether this first khipu grouping included seven or nine khipus. The 257 series contains six khipus (257A–F),

Cleaning khipus in the 257 series linked set. Photo: Adriana von Hagen.

which were all tied together at the time of their discovery (p. 66). This bundle of khipus was found in a twisted, muddied ball, and it was deemed essential, for conservation purposes, to untie two of the khipus (257A and B) from the others. Fortunately, fairly good photographic documentation of the process of untying the two khipus exists, allowing us to study the original manner in which these khipus were tied together.

What can we learn from the two groups of khipus? In the first place, since they were tied together in two separate groupings, it seems obvious that the 109 and 257 series represented some sort of collective accounting. The seven linked khipus of the 109 series include samples that are composed of 6, 13, 47, 22, 45 and 156 pendant strings, for a total of 289 strings. The two additional 109 series khipus (i.e., 109A and B) contain 27 and 84 strings, totaling 400 pendant strings on the nine 109 series khipus. As for the six khipus comprising the 257 series, these contain 20, 22, 62, 63, 69 and 176 strings, respectively, for a total string count of 412.

Two features of these total string counts are worth noting. First, the two sets of khipus are both composed of several small- to medium-sized khipus and one quite large sample. The relationship between the several smaller khipus and the larger one is not clear since the large samples do not contain the string or knot totals of their respective groups of smaller khipus. Secondly, if the 109 series included nine khipus, then these two sets of khipus contain almost exactly the same total numbers of pendant strings – i.e., 400 vs. 412. Did the two khipu groupings account for a similar number – around 400 – of objects or entities in two different recording periods, or events? For instance, perhaps the records accounted for the number of tribute payers (i.e., 400–412) among the social groups (ayllus) living in this region in pre-Hispanic times. The tribute payers may have been divided into six groups (i.e., the 257 series) on one occasion, or for one accounting purpose, and into nine groups (i.e., the 109 series) on another occasion, or for another accounting purpose.

Finally, small (3–6cm) clippings of strings from five of the khipus were sent to the AMS laboratory at the University of Arizona for radiocarbon dating. The dates obtained from these samples are listed in Appendix p. 70. One khipu (UR4) dates to about 1167 CE (Christian Era) (834+/-35 B.P.). The other four dates fall between 1582–1622 CE (419+/-36 B.P. – 379+/-34 B.P.). The first date falls within the pre-Inka time period, as the beginning of Inka civilization is usually considered to date no earlier than ca. 1450 CE. (It is unclear at the present time what status we should give to this one, very early date.) The latter range of dates fall after the 1532 Spanish Conquest, suggesting that khipu records continued to be produced and used – at least in this distant, northern region of Peru – well into the early colonial period (Urton, 2001; cf. Salomon 2002).

Whatever the nature of the data encoded in the khipus from Laguna de los Cóndores, these khipus represent a unique source of information for understanding this important ancient Andean record keeping system.

Appendix
Inventory of the khipus from Laguna de los Cóndores
(Arranged by CMA #)

UR #	CMA/INC #	AMS DATE
16	CMA-373/LC2-002	414+-35 B.P.
	CMA-380/LC2-009	
	CMA-381/LC2-010 (fragmentary)	
	CMA-383/LC2-012 (fragmentary)	
	CMA-386/LC2-015 (fragmentary)	
3	CMA-419/LC1-048	403+-35 B.P.
	CMA-421/LC1-050 (two *khipus* with same number)	
	CMA-421/LC1-050 (in photo: CMA-38/LC1-0.)	
17	CMA-480/LC1-109A	
18	CMA-480/LC1-109B	
10	CMA-480/LC1-109.1	
5	CMA-480/LC1-109.2 (two *khipus* knotted together)	
19	CMA-480/LC1-109.3	
7	CMA-480/LC1-109.4	
8	CMA-480/LC1-109.5	
20	CMA-480/LC1-109.6	
6	CMA-625/LC1-254 (previously: CMA-1889/LC1-052)	
11	CMA-628/LC1-257A	
2	CMA-628/LC1/-257B	419+-36 B.P.
12	CMA-628/LC1-257C	
13	CMA-628/LC1-257D	
14	CMA-628/LC1-257E	
15	CMA-628/LC1-257F	
4	CMA-847/LC1-476	834+-35 B.P.
9	CMA-850/LC1-479	
	CMA-854/LC1-485A	
	CMA-854/LC1-485B	
	CMA-457/LC1-086 (found with mummy #181)	
1	INC-108 (previously: INC/LDC-108/LC1-497)	379+-34 B.P.
22	INC-109 (Washed *khipu*; previously: INC/LDC/LC1-499)	
21	INC-498 (previously: INC/LDC/LC1-498)	

Lena Bjerregaard

The Museo Leymebamba Textile Catalogue

Notes to the Reader:
1. In all measurements the first number refers to the length of warp, and the second to the weft.
2. "Double" means paired warps or wefts.
3. S and Z refer to spin and ply direction. For example, "S" is a single, S-spun thread, while 2S is two Z spun yarns plied together in S direction.
4. Under technique: 2/1 means paired warp/single weft.

CMA 2062. Photo: Lena Bjerregaard.

Inventory Number: CMA 2062

Item	Tunic
Material	Cotton and camelid fiber
Ply and diameter	Warp and weft, cotton: S, 0.3–0.4mm
	Embroidery yarns: 2S, 0.4–0.5mm
	Sewing (joining seams): 2Z (×4), 0.4mm
Threads per cm	18 (double) × 9
Technique	Discontinuous warp, plain-weave; embroidery
Colors	Plain-weave, cotton: white and brown
	Embroidered: red, white, ochre and brown
Size	95 × 75cm

Description

A tunic made of two panels measuring 190 × 38cm and with a discontinuous warp. Panel I features 47cm of white, followed by 96cm of brown (extending over the shoulder) and culminating in 47cm of white, while Panel II is woven in the opposite sequence (brown, white – over the shoulder – and brown again.) Viewed from the front and the back, the tunic consists of four large alternating brown and white squares.

The tunic is finished with a 3mm-wide woven band with a diamond (eye) design border created by sewing the weft of the band into the selvedge of the band in a circular movement while weaving the band. The band has a white cotton warp (2Z) and camelid fiber weft (2S) in red, ochre and brown.

In addition, the bottom of the tunic is embellished with a 5cm-wide embroidered band (camelid fiber, 2S) in two-faced running stitch (covering the cloth on both sides to create an unbroken line on either side of the fabric). The design is of human heads wearing ear ornaments, divided by a zigzag pattern between each head.

At the shoulders and at the waist level is a 3.5cm-wide embroidered band also executed in two-faced running stitch. The designs are purely geometric, and the material is 2S camelid fiber in red, ochre and dark brown.

Along the armholes and the neck slit are traces of loop-stitch embroidery in red and ochre camelid fiber (2S).

The tunic has a small reinforcement under the neck slit on one side (3 lines of running stitch over 3cm) in cotton, 2Z (× 4). The same yarn is used for joining the panels together in the center and along the sides. In the center seam this joining is done very elegantly with overcasting stitches in white and a brown thread. These two yarns are interlocked and hold the panels together.

INVENTORY NUMBER: CMA 2065

Item	Tunic
Material	Cotton and camelid fiber
Ply and diameter	White: 1, 7, 8, 14: plain-weave, cotton, warp and weft: S, 0.3mm.
	Tapestry: camelid fiber weft: 2S, 0.4-0.5mm
	Blue: 2, 4, 6, 9, 11, and 13: warp and weft: S 0.3-0.5mm
Threads per cm	White: 1,7,8,14: plain-weave: 14 (double) × 12; tapestry: 8 (à 4) × 14-20
	Blue: 2, 4, 6, 9, 11, 13: 20 (double) × 11
Technique	Plain-weave 2/1; tapestry with a new warp shed of 4 plain-weave warps
Colors	Plain-weave, cotton: white and blue
	Tapestry weft, camelid fiber: red, rose, blue, blue-green, green, olive, khaki, ochre, black, white.
Size	95 × 86-90 cm
	White, bottom: 1, 7, 8, 14: 19 × 45cm
	White, middle: 3, 5, 10, 12: 32 × 43cm
	Blue, middle: 2, 6, 9, 13: 18 × 43cm
	Blue, shoulder pieces: 4, 11: 56.5 × 43cm

DESCRIPTION

A tunic in plain-weave and tapestry assembled from 14 separate pieces. The tunic, with the neck slit sewn shut, served as the outer wrapping of a mummy bundle and has been decorated by added embroidery stitches and damaged by moisture and mildew.

The lowest four sections (1, 7, 8, 14, counting from the lower left, continuing over the shoulder and then from lower right again over the shoulder) are white, plain-weave cotton with a 10cm-wide tapestry border in camelid fiber portraying figures reminiscent of frogs fashioned in a stunning array of colors. In typical Chachapoya fashion, they have splayed arms and legs and decorative panels on their torsos. The borders of the sections were cut across the warp at their tops and stitched tightly to the next four blue sections without folding the edges.

CMA 2065. Photo: Adriana von Hagen.

CMA 2069. Photo: Lena Bjerregaard.

The next four sections (2, 6, 9, and 13) are blue, plain-weave. They are also cut along the warp along their upper edges and sewn to the four white pieces described above.

The following four (3, 5, 10, 12) are white, plain-weave with a 9cm-wide tapestry band set slightly above waist level and adorned with figures similar to those on the bottom of the tunic, albeit somewhat smaller.

The two shoulder pieces (4, 11) are in blue plain-weave and fold over the shoulders.

Along the bottom edge of the tunic a red woven band was attached while weaving by sewing the wefts of the band into the tunic's edge.

The dimensions of this tunic, wider and longer than standard Inka tunics, along with its patchwork assembly and unique iconography suggests a Chachapoya affiliation.

Inventory Number: CMA 2069

Item	Tunic (disassembled)
Material	Cotton
Ply and diameter	Warp: S (double), 0.2-0.3mm
	Weft: S, 0.2-0.3mm
	Sewing and reinforcement thread of the original tunic: S (× 4), 0.2-0.3mm
	Thread for sewing panels together: 8Z, 0,6mm
Threads per cm	18 × 8
Technique	Plain-weave; supplementary floating warps
Colors	Three hues of reddish brown, yellow and blue
Size	Panel I: 183 × 38cm, Panel II: 187 × 38cm

Description

A tunic, which at the time of burial was taken apart and reassembled warp end to warp end (instead of weft selvedge to weft selvedge) and wrapped around the body of an adult male wearing a bone nose ornament. A complete tunic, CMA 2070; see p. 73, also accompanied the bundle.

One panel has been torn along the weft selvedge and a small strip of it is left in the original mid-seam of the other panel. The reinforcements under the neck slit and the arm holes are intact. Thus, the original tunic measured: 183-187 × 76cm. The neck slit was 33cm long as were the armholes (folded at the shoulder, making each arm hole 16.5cm long). Along the bottom, the warp selvedges have a 0.5cm-wide woven band, sewn into the tunic with the weft of the band while it was being woven.

The supplementary, floating warp pattern is fashioned from four warp layers (two crosses) Shed 1: light brown, like the sides of the pattern stripe. This shed operates normally as in plain-weave. Shed 2: double threads, dark brown and white. This shed is divided into a layer of dark brown and a layer of white. The white and the dark brown warp layers jump over three weft rows of the plain-weave, forming alternate three-span-floats on the two sides of the weaving.

INVENTORY NUMBER: CMA 2070

Item	Tunic
Material	Camelid fiber and cotton
Ply and diameter	Warp: cotton, white, blue and brown: S, 0.2-0.3mm
	Weft: cotton, white, blue and brown, S, 0.2-0.3mm
	Pattern weft: tapestry, camelid fiber, 2S, 0.5mm
	Brocade: camelid fiber, blue 2Z, 0.5mm, red: 2S, 0.5mm
	Embroidery yarns: camelid fiber, blue, ochre, white: 2Z, 0.5mm; red 2S, 0.5mm
Threads per cm	Plain-weave: 16-22 (double) × 13
	Tapestry: 7 × 36
Technique	Discontinuous warp with plain-weave 2/1; supplementary, floating warps; Tapestry, single-faced brocade and embroidery
Colors	Cotton: white, blue, brown
	Camelid fiber: red, blue, white, ochre, black
Size	98 × 79cm

Description

A tunic assembled from two panels (39-40 × 196cm) sewn together down the middle and along the sides. The bottom of the tunic is edged by a 2cm-wide fringe created by the warp threads, Z twined 4 (double) together and finished with a simple knot 0.8mm from the first weft, and ending in loose threads 1cm long. The fringe is topped by a 2cm-wide tapestry border of a volute motif with an eccentric weft and a warp composed of six plain-weave warps picked up from the plain-weave section above it. This is followed by a design of profile feline heads executed in single-faced brocade, 1.5cm wide, followed by another band of the tapestry volute design.

The brown, plain-weave sections on both sides of the tunic contain two supplementary, floating warp patterns in white and light brown. The pattern warps were inserted along the warp selvedge and then cut and secured between the two warp layers following the design field. The decorated area measures 30 × 12cm and portrays splayed supernatural beings with feline attributes such as rounded ears, prominent teeth and interlocking canines that wrap half way around the head.

The blue, plain-weave sections are decorated with 4cm-wide running and chain-stitch embroidery, forming an unbroken line in red and white camelid fiber to create a geometric, stepped design.

Just below the neck slit is a 10.5 × 7cm embroidered square panel in running stitch in blue and red camelid fiber yarn displaying a profile feline with the tail curled over the back.

The shoulders of the tunic are embellished by a 4 cm-wide band in single-faced brocade with lines in double-faced brocade. Again the design is of profile felines in blue, white, dark green, ochre and red camelid fiber.

The tunic was found with the neck slit sewn shut and had been placed over the body of an adult male wearing a bone nose ornament. It is one of five textiles that accompanied the body (See CMA 2069, p. 71).

Again, the dimensions, range of weaving structures and iconography of this tunic point to its Chachapoya affiliation. Unlike other Chachapoya tunics (e.g. CMA 2065, p. 70), assembled from many pieces, this tunic is composed of two loom panels sewn down the center and the sides, leaving openings for the arms and the neck.

CMA 2070. Photo: Adriana von Hagen.

CMA 2073. Photo: Adriana von Hagen.

INVENTORY NUMBER: CMA 2073

Item	Tunic
Material	Cotton and camelid fiber
Ply and diameter	Warp: S (double), 0.3mm
	Weft: S, 0.3mm
	Brocade, camelid fiber: 2S, 0.4-0.5mm
	Brocade, cotton: S, 0.4-0.5mm
	Sewing thread: side, middle and reinforcement: 2Z, 0.7-0.8mm
	Sewing thread, outer embroidery:
	white: 2S × 44 Z à 2S
	brown: 16 Z à 2S
Threads per cm	14 (double) × 8
Technique	Discontinuous warp plain-weave 2/1; brocade
Colors	Plain-weave, cotton: white and brown
	Brocade: camelid fiber: red, ochre, blue, brown, and olive green
	Cotton: blue, white, tan
Size	81 × 65cm

DESCRIPTION

A tunic assembled from two cotton panels woven in discontinuous warp. Panel I is formed by 37cm of white, 88cm of brown and 37cm of white cotton, while Panel II is divided into 37cm of brown, 88cm of white and 37cm of brown cloth. Thus, each side of the tunic is divided into four colors, creating a checkerboard effect, recalling CMA 2062, p. 69 and CMA 845, p. 79.

The bottom edge of the tunic is finished with a cotton band (warp faced, blue warp, white weft) sewn into the tunic while on the loom, using the weft of the band as the sewing thread.

The white sections of the tunic are decorated with 5.5cm-wide brocaded bands. The bottom band has designs in red, blue, olive green and dark brown camelid fiber of human heads wearing ear spools. The band at waist level displays geometric designs in red, brown, ochre and blue. The wefts of the brocade are camelid fiber.

The brown sections of the tunic are decorated with small brocaded squares measuring around 4.5 × 4.5cm in width. These include designs of human heads, profile felines, and geometric patterns.

The tunic is stitched together in the middle and along the sides with white/brown cotton thread. This thread was also used to reinforce the arm holes and the neck slit.

The tunic formed the outer layer of a mummy bundle and is decorated with chain-stitch embroidery that once held together the outer layers of the bundle's textiles. The bundle was topped by an embroidered, stylized human face. The embroidery thread is very fine and resembles machine-spun threads.

Inventory Number: CMA 845

Item	Tunic
Material	Cotton and camelid fiber
Ply and diameter	(side A) I a. bottom left (brown), warp: cotton, S, 0.3mm
	Weft: cotton, 2Z, 0.3mm
	I b: pattern weft: camelid fiber, 2S, 0.4-0.6mm
	II a: bottom right (white), warp: cotton, S, 0.3mm
	Weft: cotton, 2Z, 0.5mm
	II b: pattern weft: camelid fiber, 2S, 0.4-0.7mm
	III: middle panel: warp: cotton, 2.2S, 0.4mm
	Weft: camelid fiber, 2S, 0.4-0.5mm
	IV: top left, (white): warp: cotton, S, 0.3mm
	Weft: cotton, S, 0.3mm
	Pattern weft: camelid fiber, 2S, 0.5-0.6mm
	V: top right, (brown): warp: cotton, S, 0.3mm
	Weft: cotton, S 0.3mm
	Pattern weft: camelid fiber, 2S, 0.4-0.7mm
	Sewing thread; embroidery, neck, sleeves, sides and bottom: cotton, 4 Z, 1-1.5mm
	Joining of pieces, original: cotton 2Z, 0.4mm
	Repairs (blue): cotton, 2Z, 0.6mm
Threads per cm	I a: 14 (double) × 7, I b: 5 × 32
	II a: 16 (double) × 9, II b: 5 × 32
	III: 11 × 32
	IV: 20 (double) × 7
	V: 20 (double) × 7
Technique	I and II plain-weave 2/1; tapestry
	III: slit, dovetailed and interlocked tapestry
	IV: plain-weave 1/1; negative and two-faced brocade
	V: plain-weave 1/1; two-faced brocade.
Colors	Cotton: brown, white
	Camelid fiber: red, blue, brown, dark yellow-ochre, light yellow-ochre, green, rose, black
Size	85 × 70cm

Description

A tunic composed of seven pieces sewn together. The bottom of the tunic is finished with four sets of weavings (two in front, two in back, 33 × 34-35cm) executed with vertical warps and producing a border design that resembles splayed arms and legs, viewed sideways. This design suposedly represents frogs (María Jesús Ximénes Diaz, personal communication). This tapestry border was achieved by using a new shed (2/2 double) from the plain-weave that serves as its basis.

The waist band is formed by a single tapestry band (140 × 14cm) with a horizontal warp. It portrays a series of hybrid beings in an array of colors with splayed arms and legs, noses shaped like clothes pegs, curlicued ears and a variety of designs, mainly diamond-shaped checkerboards, on their torsos.

The two top sections (74 × 33-34cm) have vertical warps and discontinuous warp-joining at the shoulders. In the white sections they both display anthropomorphic heads arrayed in a step pattern and executed in negative brocade framed by a stripe in two-faced brocade. In the brown sections the tunic is embellished with a fearsome supernatural figure with prominent teeth, created in two-faced brocade.

The neck, armholes and bottom edge of the tunic are finished with loop-stitch embroidery in dark and light brown, although the original colors are difficult to distinguish. The tunic is sewn along the sides with figure-eight stitching in groups of three, also in light brown.

The tunic shows signs of wear and the joins between the pieces and sections of dovetail tapestry were repaired with a variety of colored threads.

This tunic is a classic example of the hybrid Chachapoya-Inka style. Several features point to its Inka affiliation: its size (85 × 75cm) falls within the range of known

CMA 845. Photo: Adriana von Hagen.

Inca tunics At the same time, the tapestry waist band is a common trait in provincial Inka tunics, as is the checkerboard quality of the contrasting brown and white panels and the cross-knit loop-stitching along the bottom edge of the tunic and the figure-eight stitching along the sides. Other features such as the patchwork assembly of the piece (in this case, seven pieces sewn together) as well as the mix of weaving structures (two types of brocade, three of tapestry, embroidery and plain-weave); however, are hallmarks of the Chachapoya style. Finally, the iconography is classically Chachapoya.

CMA 756. Photo: Adriana von Hagen.

INVENTORY NUMBER: CMA 756

Item	Tunic
Material	Cotton
Ply and diameter	Warp: S, 0.3mm
	Weft: S, 0.3mm
	Edgings (arm holes, bottom, original side stitches): 2Z (double).
	Repair yarns: 2Z, 1.2-2mm
	Repair patch: warp: S, 0.3mm
	Neck slit closure: 6Z, 0.3mm
Threads per cm	12-14 (double) × 7
	Repair patch: 16 (double) × 7
Technique	Plain-weave 2/1 with applied pigment
Colors	Warp and weft: tan
	Painted pattern: medium and dark brown
Size	83 × 70cm

DESCRIPTION

A plain-weave, painted cotton tunic woven as one piece (vertical warp) with divided wefts along the 38cm-long neck slit. The tunic has 3 × 2Z headings at the top and bottom ends and the final joining of the weaving was done with double and triple wefts over 2cm – one cm from the bottom edge on the best preserved face of the tunic. Fragments of loop-stitch embroidery can be observed on the neck slit, arm holes and the bottom edge of the tunic. The tunic is so worn that the cotton is very supple. It has been extensively repaired with patches (in plain-weave 2/1 cotton) and darning in coarse 2S cotton thread.

Each side of the tunic (one side is missing a large fragment) is arrayed with Chachapoya-style human figures wearing earspools and some sort of headgear (perhaps plumed headdresses?) that extend from the tops and sides of the heads. The figures are framed within irregular squares and the freehand, spontaneous design contrasts with the rigid geometric motifs seen on tunic CMA 569, p. 82. The paint, in two hues of brown, was probably applied as a thick paste of mineral pigments as the color has not saturated the fabric.

The sewn neck slit indicates that this tunic covered a body or served as the outer wrapping of a mummy bundle.

Inventory Number: CMA 394

Item	Tunic
Material	Cotton and camelid fiber
Ply and diameter	Warp: cotton: S (double), 0.3-0.4mm
	Weft: cotton: S, 0.5mm
	Pattern: camelid fiber: 2S, 0.6-0.7mm
Threads per cm	20-26 × 9
Technique	Discontinuous warp face; plain-weave; two-faced brocade; chain-stitch embroidery
Colors	Plain-weave: beige and blue
	Patterning: red, ochre, blue and brown
Size	Approx. 93 × 75cm

Description

A tunic consisting of two panels sewn together along the front and sides. Each panel is made up of 18cm of beige plain-weave cotton with 10cm of brocade at the bottom; 20cm of plain-weave in blue; 15cm of plain-weave in beige with a 6.5cm-wide band of brocade patterning in the center; 18cm of blue plain-weave; 15cm of beige plain-weave with 6cm of brocade in the middle; and 14cm of blue plain-weave that continues over the shoulders. The color sequence repeats itself in the opposite order on the other side. The armholes measure 22cm and the neck slit 36cm. The bottom of the tunic is edged with a narrow warp-faced weaving (0.7cm) with a red camelid fiber warp and a beige cotton weft that at each shift of the shed had been sewn into the tunic's edge. The tunic is sewn together with very small stem-stitches using the same yarn as the weft. The brocade patterning includes a series of profile felines in red and blue adorning the bottom of the tunic, the waistband and near the shoulders. The tunic was found wrapped around the neck of the mummy of an adult male. The bundle, which had been slashed by looters, also contained a pair of copper tweezers, a blue stone bead and shell beads attached to a cotton cord.

CMA 394. Photo: Adriana von Hagen.

Warp direction →

Inventory Number: INCL 111

Item	Tunic
Material	Cotton and camelid fiber
Ply and diameter	Warp, cotton: 3Z, 0.7mm
	Weft, camelid fiber: 2S, 0.5mm
Threads per cm	10 × 30
Technique	Dovetailed (2/2) tapestry; loop-stitch embroidery
Colors	Warp: white
	Weft: red, white, ochre, black, light tan, medium tan
Size	75 × 136cm

Description

Fragment of a tapestry tunic with a horizontal warp, woven on an upright loom. Judging from the remains of the fabric, the original loom panel measured 75 × ca. 192cm or about 75 × 96cm as worn.

The warp selvedges are inter-looped at both ends and traces of the original loop-stitch embroidery are present both at the neck and the arm holes as well as at the bottom edge of the tunic. Along the sides there are also traces of an embroidered joining. This edging and joining is done in 2S white, red and ochre camelid fiber.

The tunic is patterned with a series of stylized human heads and profile felines with prominent teeth and interlocking canines. Each head is framed in a square, ranging from 5.5 × 5.5 to 6 × 6cm. On the shoulders, where the heads change direction, the squares extend to 5.5 × 8cm. The squares are arrayed in a diamond pattern around the neck slit, creating a step-like design on the front (most of which is preserved) of the tunic (most of the back is missing). Every second row the design within the square changes from human to feline.

The fill color between the design squares is red and tan, separated in the middle. Starting with 45cm of red/tan (running along the weft) 37.5cm (half the width of the tunic), then switching colors so that tan lies above the red and red over the tan. This color pattern continues over the shoulders and probably for 102cm, and then, no doubt, the colors alternated again, to match the front of the tunic. As the back is fragmented it is not possible to state this with certainty.

The bottom of the tunic is edged with a 10cm-wide border composed of two different human heads wearing elaborate headdresses and ear ornaments (only 20cm of the border design have been preserved, so it is impossible to discern if the border included more designs or just the two alternating heads).

The dimensions of the tunic (although somewhat longer than standard provincial Inca tunics), the tapestry weave (reserved for the highest quality tunics), the checkerboard effect of the design, the remains of loop-stitch embroidery, and the fact that the tunic was woven on an upright loom point to Inca influence, but the design motifs are quintessentially Chachapoya. This tunic was not found at the Laguna de los Cóndores LC1 *chullpa* site, the provenance of the majority of the Museo Leymebamba's textiles. Rather, it is said to come from a looted burial site on cliffs located to the north of the lake.

INCL 111. Photo: Lena Bjerregaard.

CMA 569. Photo: Lena Bjerregaard.

Inventory Number: CMA 569

Item	Tunic
Material	Cotton
Ply and diameter	Warp: Z (double), 0.3–0.8mm (irregular, mainly 0.3–0.5mm)
	Weft: Z (double), 0.3–0.5mm
	Thread closing neck opening: 4Z, 0.3mm
Threads per cm	10 (double) × 6
Technique	Plain-weave (2/2) with applied pigment
Colors	Warp, weft, embroidery and sewing: cream/light tan
	Pigment: blue-grey, three shades of brown
Size	139 × 50cm

Description

Fragment of a one piece, painted tunic. The neck opening is 35cm from the side selvedge, which indicates that the complete piece measured 70cm in width, falling within the known range of Inca tunic widths.[1] The fragment is decorated with a horizontal design 6.5cm wide at the shoulder level and with two additional stripes at 38cm on either side of the shoulder. The rest of the painted design covers the whole fragment.[2] The tunic is made of Z-spun cotton, an uncommon trait among the Laguna de los Cóndores textiles. The tunic may have been imported to the region from the coast or the tropical lowlands. Because the neck opening has been sewn shut and there are traces of cotton thread dotting the fragment (the remains of zigzag embroidery), the tunic probably covered a body and may have formed the outer wrapping of a mummy bundle.

CMA 2082. Photo: Lena Bjerregaard.

Inventory number: CMA 2082

Item	Woman's dress
Material	Cotton, wool and human hair
Ply and diameter	Warp, cotton: 2S, 0.15-0.2mm
	Weft, wool: 2S, 0.15 – 0.2mm
	Embroidery and braid, cotton: 6S, 0.4mm
	Chain stitch edging: wool, 2S, 0.5mm
	Joining in 8 stitches: wool, 2S, 0.5mm
Threads per cm	20 × 120
Technique	Weft faced plain-weave
	Embroidery (soumak) and braid
Colours	Warp: tan
	Weft: dark brown, tan, red
	Embroidery and braid: white
Size	151 × 175cm

Description

A very fine (possibly vicuña) woman's wrap-around dress sewn together from two panels. The weaving has chained warp loops indicating that it is weft faced plain-weave. It is dark brown in the middle and at the top and bottom has a 23cm-wide tan stripe that every 5,5cm has a 0,5cm-wide red stripe. Along the top and bottom the cloth is cut along a weft stripe, folded twice and a woollen loop stitch embroidery edge finishes the panels. This loop stitch embroidery is also used to cover the warp selvages. This edge embroidery only exists fragmentarily today.

These two warp selvages are joined together by an 8 shaped embroidery done in a dark brown woollen thread.

The wrap-around dress is similar to the Inka wrapped dresses excavated by Uhle from the cemetery of the sacrificed women at Pachacamac (Uhle 1903).

The wrap-around dress was used as outer wrapping of a woman's mummy bundle and a stylized human face is embroidered onto it with a thick white cotton yarn indicating where the mummy's head was. On top of the mummy is a 4-braid also in thick, white cotton yarn attached. The braid is 19cm long; on the upper 10cm it has human hair braided in. After the braiding is a looped simple knot and the loose ends of the 4 yarns hang loose another 14cm – making braid and loose ends 43cm in all.

Inventory Number: INCL 112

Item	Mantle
Material	Cotton
Ply and diameter	Warp: S, 0.3-0.5mm
	Weft: S, 0.3mm
Threads per cm	14 (double) × 6
Headings	Finishing end 1 × 6, 4 × 2, 4 × 6, 4 × 2; starting end: 1 × 4, 2 × 2.
Technique	Warp faced plain-weave (2/1) with floating warps

CMA 112. Photo: Adriana von Hagen.

Warp direction ⟶

Colors	Orange, rose, green, blue, light blue, white, ochre
Size	190 × 155. (3 panels, 52cm, 52cm and 51cm, respectively)

DESCRIPTION

Large mantle composed of three loom panels sewn together. The weaving has an orange/brown basis and is decorated with warp stripes of differing widths ranging from a few mm to 4cm. Some of the warp stripes have supplementary, floating warps that consistently skip three wefts. These floating warp stripes have geometric patterns.

INVENTORY NUMBER: CMA 600

Item	Mantle or tunic
Material	Cotton
Ply and diameter	Warps: S, 0.2-0.5mm
	Wefts: S, 0.2-0.3mm
	Pattern weft, brocade: 2Z, 0.5mm
	Sewing thread: 3Z, 0.8-1mm
Threads per cm	22 (double) × 11
Technique	Plain-weave (2/1); tie-dyed plain-weave; brocade
Colors	Tan, white, orange-red, dark brown, medium brown and blue
Size	Fragment I: 18 × 39 cm, fragment II: 58 × 39cm, fragment III: 51 × 39cm
	Fragment IV: 56 × 41cm

DESCRIPTION

Four fragments, each sewn together along weft selvedges from six strips (4.5cm; 3.5cm; 4.5cm; 3.5cm; 3.5cm; 19cm, respectively). The strips were dyed in a variety of colors. Three of the strips (2 × 4.5cm; 1 × 3.5cm) are decorated with a tie-dye pattern of small circles. In the middle of the 19cm strip there is a 1cm to 2-4cm-wide brocaded stripe (orange on white) embellished with anthropomorphic heads and geometric patterns, and 1.5cm from the side selvedges there are narrow (1.5-4mm) warp stripes in blue, orange and cream.

Fragment I (the smallest) has a warp end cut across the warp, rolled twice and sewn. Alongside the blue stripe are traces of an extra piece of material. Fragment II (the middle one) has a seam across the warp, joining the two panels together along the warp. All the warp ends (except the one 19cm stripe facing Fragment I, which is a warp selvedge) are cut, rolled and sewn. Fragments I and II (above the warp-seam) display the same pattern on the brocade and they probably belong to the same textile. Although Fragments II and III (below the warp-seam) share the same pattern, this is not the same as the one on Fragment I.

There are traces of some additional material that had been attached along the sides of the panels. Along one

CMA 600. Photo: Adriana von Hagen.

side of Fragment II there is a 27cm-long, thick SZ twined blue string sewn on to the edge of the last stripe as well as traces of more material attached to these 27cm on both sides. Fragment III also has traces of more material sewn on along one side. At the bottom, the 19 cm stripe has a beginning warp selvedge, and two of the narrower strips have been cut, folded twice and sewn. The other strips are fragmented.

Fragment IV is 2cm wider than the others. The brocade pattern is different from the other two panels and it has narrow stripes with supplementary, floating warps while the other two have plain warp stripes. The textile is cut across the warp, folded twice and sewn like the other panels.

Thus the four fragments – three of them with finished edges – do not appear to have formed part of the same garment, although they are very similar.

In addition, the occurrence of tie-dye is rare among the Laguna de los Cóndores textiles. These four fragments and a small, blue tie-dyed bag are the only examples of the technique registered at the Museo Leymebamba. A mummy bundle from the Chachapoya site of Laguna Huayabamba yielded a tie-dyed, plain-weave cotton textile.[3] Thus far, these and a tunic from Quintecocha, which neighbors Laguna de los Cohndores, are the only known examples from the Chachapoya heartland.

The fragments may have been part of a mantle – similar fragments from Ancón and Paramonga are in the Ethnologisches Museum in Berlin. Unfortunately, the piece is too fragmented to determine its original function.

Inventory Number: CMA 2257

Item	Mantle
Material	Cotton
Ply and diameter	Warp: S, 0.3-0.5mm
	Weft: S, 0.4mm
	Sewing threads: 3 Z, 0.7mm
Threads per cm	14 (double) × 8
Headings	Beginning: 4, 3 × 2; end: 6, 3 × 2, 3 × 4, and 2 × 2
Technique	Warp faced plain-weave (2/1); warp stripes ranging from 0.2-2.6cm in width. Three of the widest stripes have supplementary, floating warps (over three wefts).
Colors	White, light blue, dark blue/green, rose, black and brown
Size	119 × 78 cm; cut and sewn from one piece (238 × 38cm)

Description

This mantle, originally woven as one piece measuring 238 × 38cm, was subsequently cut down the center (across the warp) and sewn together along two side selvedges. The pieces are stitched together in such a way that each end of the mantle consists of one cut, and one selvedge end. This seam appears to be original, as the thread is faded on one side and not on the other, matching the fading apparent on one side of the mantle. The floating warp stripes feature motifs of stylized human heads, profile felines and geometric designs.

CMA 2257. Photo: Adriana von Hagen.

Warp direction ⟶

Inventory Number: CMA 397

Item	Belt
Material	Camelid fiber
Ply and diameter	Warp: 2S, 0.6mm
	Weft: 2S, 0.6mm
Threads per cm	36 × 8
Technique	Complementary warp
Colors	Warp: cream, tan, medium brown, dark brown
	Weft: dark brown
Size	457 × 3-3.5cm

Description

Twelve fragments of a camelid fiber band woven in four shades of brown and decorated with geometric designs. The center piece (1cm) is tan/medium brown, while the two sides (each 1cm) are cream/dark brown. In various places the band has traces of red/orange edging on both sides of the patterning, probably the remains of a 0.5cm-wide edge stripe, a common feature of Inka-style belts and the straps of small bags. The belt was found wrapped around the waist of an adolescent girl. Many of the Laguna de los Cóndores mummies are cinched with similar style belts.

CMA 397. Photo: Lena Bjerregaard.

CMA 391. Photo: Adriana von Hagen.

INVENTORY NUMBER: CMA 391

Item	Band with fringe
Material	Camelid fiber and cotton
Ply and diameter	Warp, cotton: 3Z, 0.5mm
	Weft, camelid fiber: 2S, 0.4-0.5mm
Threads per cm	7 × 40
Technique	Tapestry; open work; fringe of four superimposed tassels
Colors	Warp, cotton: cream
	Weft, camelid fiber: brown, red and yellow
Size	150 × 6cm (in eight fragments). Fringe: 8cm (consisting of four tassels each measuring 3cm and placed on top of each other.

DESCRIPTION

A band consisting of 2cm of tapestry weave with a step design in red, ochre and brown followed by 1cm of open work (wefts only) and a 2cm weft fringe of two, Z-twined wefts. One of the fragments has an 8cm-long tassel. The fringed band may have embellished the bottom edge of a tunic.

INVENTORY NUMBER: CMA 425

Item	Belt
Material	Cotton and camelid fiber
Ply and diameter	Warp and weft: cotton, 2S, 0.5-0.7mm
	Pattern weft: camelid fiber, 2S (double), 0.5-0.7mm
Threads per cm	Plain-weave: 28 × 8
Technique	Plain-weave 1/1; lancé (edge to edge single-faced brocade)
Colors	Plain-weave: undyed light tan, patterning: red
Size	50cm (in three fragments: 15cm, 15cm and 20cm, respectively) × 4.5cm

Description

Three fragments of a plain-weave, warp-faced belt decorated with 3.5-4.5 cm-wide lancé patterns. Seven of the patterns are diamonds starting with floats under one and over five warps. The last motif, close to the warp selvedge, includes an irregular zigzag pattern under one or two, and over two-three-four warps. This warp end has 0.7mm loops at the end, and one still retains a piece of the cord (2Z, 3mm) that tied it to the loom bar.

Inventory Number: INCL 97

Item	Head band
Material	Camelid fiber, cotton, and plant fiber
Ply and diameter	Camelid fiber (cut pile) Z, 1mm
	Cotton (pile attachment yarns) 2Z, 0.6-0.8mm
	Plain-weave 1. warp and weft: S, 0.3mm
	2. Warp and weft: S, 0.2mm
Threads per cm	Plain-weave 1: 12 (double) × 10
	2: 13 × 13
Technique	Furred cord and plain-weave.
Colors	Red and tan
Size	54cm (circumference)

Description

A furred head ornament composed of a circular core of unspun plant fibers (4cm wide, 5cm high and with a diameter of 24cm) covered by two types of plain-weave cotton material. The outer layer is the customary 2/1, while the inner one is a fine 1/1 very light, open weave.

The head ornament was covered by a 1cm-long fringe of red camelid fiber held in place with two twisted white cotton strings. This very long fringe was then stitched to the outside of the ring of plant fiber covered by plain woven cotton material.

CMA 425. Photo: Lena Bjerregaard.

INCL 97. Photo: Adriana von Hagen.

Inventory Number: CMA 676

Item	Tunic waist band (?) (fragment)
Material	Camelid fiber and cotton
Ply and diameter	Warp, cotton: 3Z, 1mm
	Weft, camelid fiber: 2S, 0.7-0.8mm
Threads per cm	7 × 28-30
Technique	Interlocked and dovetailed tapestry
Colors	Warp: white
	Weft: red, white, black, purple, ochre, green, brown and orange.
Size	80 × 9cm

Description

A fragmented piece of tapestry with parts of both weft selvedges intact.

The decoration includes designs of felines, hybrid creatures, human heads and front-facing figures set in groups of two to three and framed by a black line. The fragment may have formed the waist band of a tunic.

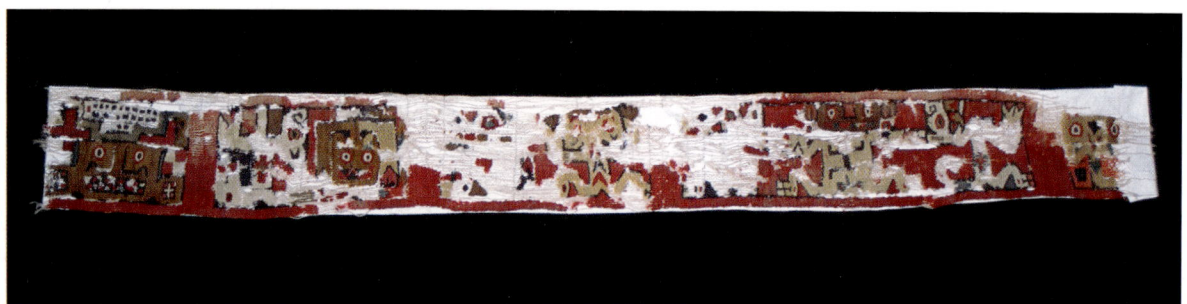

CMA 676. Photo: Adriana von Hagen.

CMA 1832. Photo: Adriana von Hagen.

INVENTORY NUMBER: CMA 1832

Item	Head band
Material	Cotton, camelid fiber and shell beads
Ply and diameter	Warp: 3 Z, 0.5mm
	Weft: red: 2S, blue: 2Z, 0.5mm
	Sewing thread: 3Z, 0.5mm
	Tying yarn 1: 2S, 0.1mm; 2: 14Z, 3mm
Threads per cm	10 × 36
Technique	Tapestry; flat shell beads sewn on to the band
Colors	Weft: red, blue
	Warp: white
	Tying yarns: white and tan
	Beads: white
Size	58 × 2cm Shell beads: 4mm wide, 0.3-0.5mm thick.

DESCRIPTION

A narrow, 50cm-long band in tapestry weave patterned with blue and red triangles. Small, white shell beads have been embroidered onto the outside of the band, following the zigzag line of the tapestry pattern and the outside edges of the band.

The band is tied with a thick, white cotton yarn 8cm long, bringing the total length of the band to 58cm. An 8cm-long cotton string is attached to one end. It has two complex knots, one around a shell, and a simple end knot.

CMA 1834. Photo: Lena Bjerregaard.

INVENTORY NUMBER: CMA 1834

Item	Head band
Material	Plant fiber, cotton, human hair
Ply and diameter	Tying yarn: 2S, 0.3-0.2mm
Technique	Furred cord
Colors	Tying threads: white/grey
	Black human hair
Size	54cm

DESCRIPTION

A headband formed over a core of unspun plant fibers. A furred cord, created by a fringe of human hair secured by two twisted cotton cords, has been wrapped around the core. At the back, the headband has a 3cm-long simple cotton cord and a white, double 2Z cotton yarn that winds around the core of plant fiber.

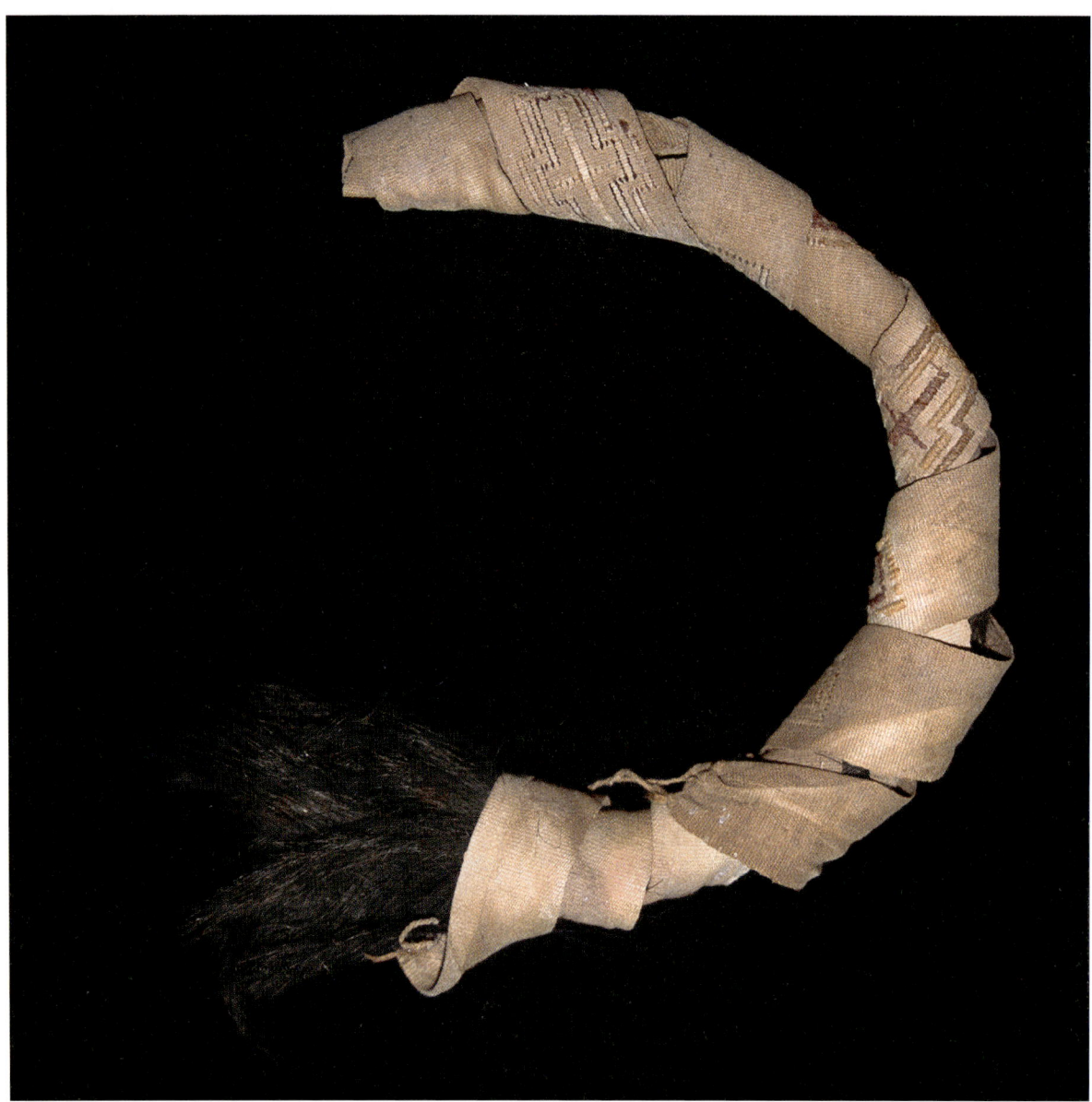

CMA 516. Photo: Adriana von Hagen.

Inventory Number: CMA 516

Item	Band
Material	Cotton and camelid fiber; human hair
Ply and diameter	Warp and weft, cotton: 2S, 0.3–0.5mm
	Pattern weft, camelid fiber (red, tan): 2S 0.4–0.5mm
	Pattern weft, camelid fiber (ochre): 2Z, 0.5mm
Threads per cm	38 × 12
Technique	Warp faced plain-weave; two-faced brocade
Colors	Plain-weave: tan
	Brocade: tan, ochre, red
Size	Approx. 150 × 3.5cm

Description

A long band decorated with five cross-like patterns in two-faced brocade (each measuring 6 × 3cm). The band is wrapped around a tuft of human hair, 29cm long. The brocade patterns are found only on the first half of the band, which is wrapped around the hair, so that the brocaded designs are on the outside of the band. The band has a 14cm-long 2.2S yarn attached to the start heading and is cut and sewn with stem-stitches across the other warp end. The band and tuft of human hair were found in the mummy bundle of an adult male and probably belonged to the man contained in the bundle.

Inventory Number: CMA 768

Item	Band (fragment)
Material	Cotton
Ply and diameter	Warp, weft and sewing thread: 2Z, 0.4mm
Threads per cm	32 × 6
Technique	Tubular weaving; complementary warp patterning
Colors	Beige, medium brown and dark brown
Size	7 × 2cm

Description

Tubular weaving with complementary warp patterning in both layers of the weaving. At both ends of the band there is an unpatterned, 2mm-wide edge, that continues over to the other side. The patterned part (1.6mm) interchanges layers of the two sides of the band every 1.2cm. The design is composed of 12 × 8mm squares with horizontal stripes, zigzags and circles.

At the warp end of the band is a row of loop-stitches, made of four strands of thread similar to the warp and the weft.

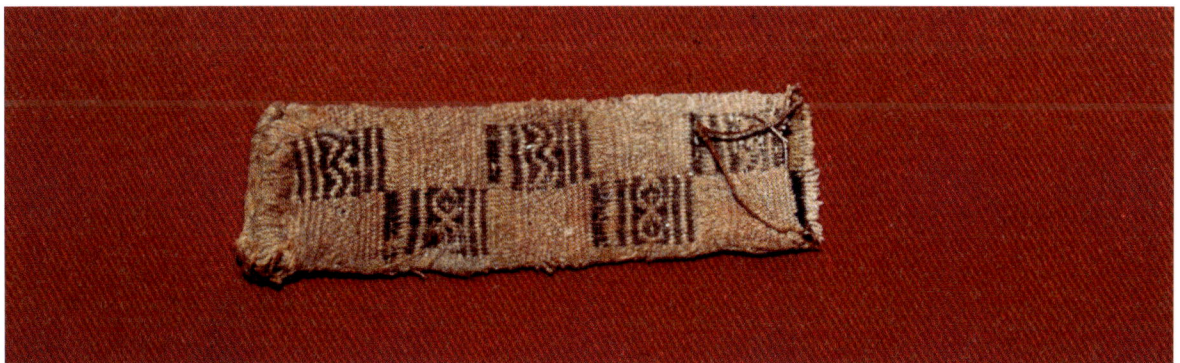

CMA 768. Photo: Lena Bjerregaard.

CMA 834 (see also p. 61). Photo: Adriana von Hagen.

Inventory Number: CMA 834

Item	Bag
Material	Cotton and camelid fiber
Ply and diameter	Warp, cotton: 3 S-0.5 mm
	Weft, camelid fiber: 2 S-0.3 mm
	Fringe, warp, camelid fiber: 2Z-7S-2Z - 2 mm
	Weft, cotton: 6Z
Threads per cm	9 × 40
Technique	Interlocked tapestry; the warp-ends are braided along both warp selvedges
Colors	Warp: white/tan
	Weft: yellow ochre, light ochre, red, green, white and brown.
Size	19 × 21cm; fringe: 3-4cm

Description

A bag assembled from a single piece of tapestry with a horizontal warp and folded at the bottom. Along the sides (warp selvedges) the warps are braided. At the bottom is a fringe of thick camelid fiber Z-plied yarns ending in two knots and held together at the top by two cotton warps. Both sides of the bag portray images of two splayed human figures, in red, with inverted, T-shaped noses, in white, and sporting plumed headdresses. The figures are bordered by a motif of stepped triangles. The splayed stance of the figures as well as their plumed headgear and inverted T-shaped noses are typically Chachapoya in style.

CMA 407. Photo: Adriana von Hagen.

INVENTORY NUMBER: CMA 407

Item	Bag
Material	Plant fiber
Ply and diameter	Z, 2-3mm
Width of loop bands	1.5-2cm
Technique	Simple looping
Colors	Natural tan
Size	Circumference: 24cm; height from mid-bottom to top edge: 11cm

DESCRIPTION

Small bag executed in simple looping. The top of the bag has three wrapped strings that served as handles.

CMA 523. Photo: Lena Bjerregaard.

INVENTORY NUMBER: CMA 523

Item	Bag
Material	Plant fiber
Ply and diameter	Z, 2-3mm
Width of loop bands	2cm
Technique	Simple looping
Colors	Natural brown
Size	80 (from bottom center to top edge) × 72cm (width at top edge)

DESCRIPTION

A large bag in simple looping. At the top edge is a row of loose loop-stitches – 2cm between each stitch – that served as loops for attaching a carrying cord.

CMA 827. Photo: Adriana von Hagen.

Inventory Number: CMA 827

Item	Bag
Material	Camelid fiber and cotton
Ply and diameter	Weft, cotton: 3S
	Warp, camelid fiber: 2S
Threads per cm	34 × 8
Technique	Warp-faced plain-weave; complementary warp face; embroidery
Colors	Weft: white
	Warp: medium brown, red, yellow
	Embroidery: dark brown, yellow, red
Size	20 × 17

Description

This bag was probably woven as one piece, folded at the bottom, and sewn together with loop-stitching along the sides. The bag is fragmented at the bottom. It is typically Inca in style.

Inventory Number: CMA 671

Item	Bag
Material	Camelid fiber
Ply and diameter	Warp, weft, and embroidery yarns: 2S, 0.4mm
Threads per cm	36 × 8
Technique	Bag: warp-faced plain-weave; loop-stitch embroidery
	Strap: tubular weaving; complementary warp patterning
Colors	Weft: brown
	Warp: dark brown, light brown, black, white, red and yellow
Size	Bag: 19 × 19cm; strap: 71 × 3cm

Description

The strap is made as a tubular weaving. The edges (0.5cm) of the strap are red on one side and blue on the other and the middle 2cm is woven in two layers of complementary warp. Every 1 or 2cm these two layers interchange (one is dark brown/white, and the other is dark brown/yellow). The pattern is geometric (two circles and horizontal stripes).

The bag is woven in a warp-faced plain-weave with vertical stripes. It also has a few (one-three) horizontal stripes (dots). One of the yarns in the stripes is twined from a red and a white thread, resembling a barber pole.

The sides of the bag are finished with a 0.7cm-wide loop-stitch using all the colors seen in the bag.

The bag is classically Inka in style and may have been exchanged as a gift.[4]

CMA 671. Photo: Lena Bjerregaard.

CMA 673. Photo: Adriana von Hagen.

Inventory Number: CMA 673

Item	Bag
Material	Cotton
Ply and diameter	2S, 0.6mm
Loops per cm	Vertical: 9, horizontal: 6
Technique	Simple looping
Colors	Blue
Size	15 × 14cm

Description

A small bag made in a simple looping technique composed of successive bands 1.7cm wide. The bands run horizontally and the thicker lines across the bag occur where a new band was inserted. The top band has a special patterning made of two individual bands the length of the width of the bag. All the other bands are circular.

Inventory Number: CMA 684

Item	Bag
Material	Camelid fiber, cotton (top loop seam and attachment for sandal), leather (sandal) Plant fiber (sandal)
Ply and diameter	Warp: 2S, 0.6mm
	Weft: 2S, 0.8mm
	Cotton top loops: 2.2Z, 2mm
	Cotton attachment yarn: 2Z, 1mm
	Sandal: camelid fiber: 2S, 3mm, plant fiber: 2S, 1.5 mm
Threads per cm	Bag: 30 × 7
	Strap: 34 × 7
Technique	Bag: warp-faced plain-weave; stem-stitch embroidery
	Strap: complimentary warp patterning
Colors	Black, dark brown, brown, white, red, grey and ochre
Size	13 × 11cm. Strap 45 × 2cm (fragmented)

Description

A striped bag edged with zigzag stem-stitch embroidery in white, ochre, reddish brown and dark brown along the edges and a warp patterned strap with geometric designs in black, brown and white and 0.4-0.5mm-wide red stripes along the edges.

The bag has a row of loose loop-stitches at the top (for closing). One cm from the top edge is an attachment yarn holding a 4cm-long camelid fiber tassel with black, white, red and ochre threads. At the opposite corner a miniature leather sandal (8 × 4cm) was attached with camelid fiber and plant fiber yarns.

Like CMA 671, p. 99, this bag is classically Inka in style.

CMA 684. Photo: Adriana von Hagen.

CMA 730. Photo: Lena Bjerregaard.

CMA 796. Photo: Adriana von Hagen.

INVENTORY NUMBER: CMA 730

Item	Bag
Material	Plant fiber
Ply and diameter	Z, 2-3mm
Width of loop bands	1.5cm
Technique	Simple looping
Colors	Tan
Size	Circumference: 47cm; height from mid-bottom to top border: 19cm

DESCRIPTION

A plant fiber bag in simple looping with four loops (10-11cm long) on the sides that served as handles. The handles were made by tightly wrapping three strands of fibers.

The bag contains a few pieces of charcoal and a leaf that resembles a coca leaf.

INVENTORY NUMBER: CMA 796

Item	Small bag
Material	Plant fiber
Ply and diameter	Z, 0.6-1mm
Threads per cm:	–
Technique	Simple looping
Colors	Natural brown
Size	8cm (bottom to top) × 10cm (width at top)

DESCRIPTION

Small bag of looped plant fiber. At a distance of 2cm from the top the bag has a 1.2cm-wide pattern of slanting lines. The top edge has traces of two, 4S plied loops for closing.

INVENTORY NUMBER: CMA 606

Item	Bag
Material	Cotton and camelid fiber
Ply and diameter	Warp: cotton, 2S, 0.4mm
	Weft: camelid fiber, 2S, 0.4mm
Threads per cm	9 × 32
Technique	Warp faced plain-weave; warp patterning; stem-stitches.
Colors	White, dark brown and red
Size	16 × 13cm

DESCRIPTION

Bag with geometric designs. The bag was woven as one piece and folded along one side. The two sides and the bottom are edged in red, white and brown with a diamond design.

CMA 606. Photo: Adriana von Hagen.

INVENTORY NUMBER: CMA 2078

Item	Bag
Material	Cotton
Ply and diameter	3 Z, 1mm
Loops per cm	Four horizontal, four vertical
Technique	Simple looping
Colors	Mainly brown, with traces of red and blue
Size	14 × 22cm (at base)

DESCRIPTION

Looped bag made in circular stripes. The looping is shaped to make a rounded triangular form, and has a single strip (0.8mm) of double twisted loops as patterning 1.5cm from the bottom (base).

The colors have faded into various shades of brown, but traces of different colored stripes can still be seen.

The bag has a 4cm loop pulled from the looping yarn on one side, and a 45cm-long string attached on the other side.

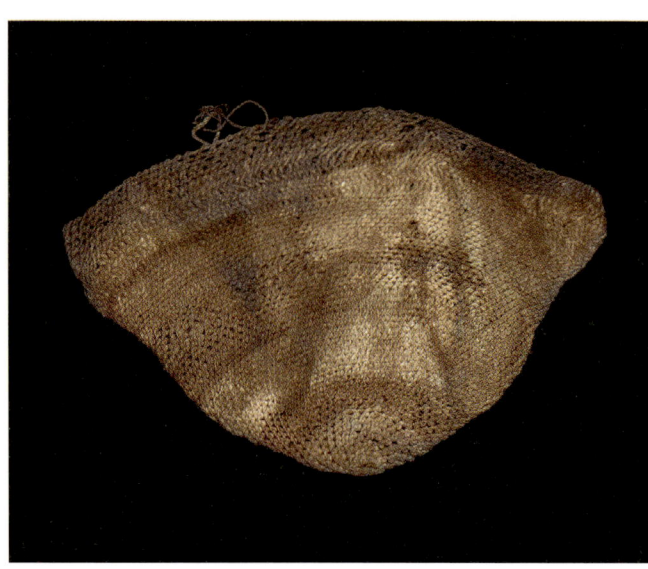

CMA 2078. Photo: Adriana von Hagen.

CMA 2084. Photo: Lena Bjerregaard.

INVENTORY NUMBER: CMA 2084

Item	Bag
Material	Cotton
Ply and diameter	Tan: warp Z; weft S
	Blue: warp and weft S
Threads per cm	Tan: 10 (dbl.)x 10
	Blue: 7 (dbl.) x 9
Technique	Plain weave 2/1. Tie dye design.
Colors	Tan and blue
Size	39 x 33,5 cm

DESCRIPTION

The bag is sewn from two pieces of cloth folded at the bottom and stitched along the sides and the middle of the bag. The blue cloth has tie dye patterns – along with CMA 600, the only other tie-dye example in the Leymebamba collection.

Both pieces are in plain weave with double warp.

The two top corners are tied with a coarse cotton string 4 times stretched from one corner to the other and probably used as a handle. This string once formed part of a quipu. It consists of a pendant with 2 knots (long knot 9Z and single knot Z) with a secondary string with 2 knots (long knots 8Z and 4Z) and a tertiary string with 1 knot (longknot 6 Z).

INCL 102. Photo: Lena Bjerregaard.

INVENTORY NUMBER: INCL 102

Item	Net
Material	Cotton
Ply and diameter	3Z, 0.8-1mm
Knots per cm	2
Technique	Simple knotting
Colors	Dark brown and cream
Size	54 × 23cm (at top)

DESCRIPTION

A knotted, cylinder-shaped net. It is knotted flat, and at the end looped together lengthwise. The net has two dark brown horizontal stripes (3.2 and 3.8cm wide, respectively).

At the wider end the net has loops, probably for pulling a yarn through for closing. The loose ends of the net yarn (12 and 27cm) dangle from the top of the net, where the joining is, and another loose yarn (39cm) is slipped into a top loop 6cm to the side of the joining.

INVENTORY NUMBER: CMA 712

Item	Net
Material	Plant fiber
Ply and diameter	3Z, 0.5mm
Distance between knots	20cm
Technique	Knotting
Colors	Natural tan
Size	106cm

DESCRIPTION

A knotted net with a very large mesh. The cords of the net are wrapped half way around circular handles at either end of the net. Attached to one of the handles is a 2-3mm Z plant fiber sewn closely with loop-stitches. It probably served as a carrying net.

CMA 712. Photo: Lena Bjerregaard.

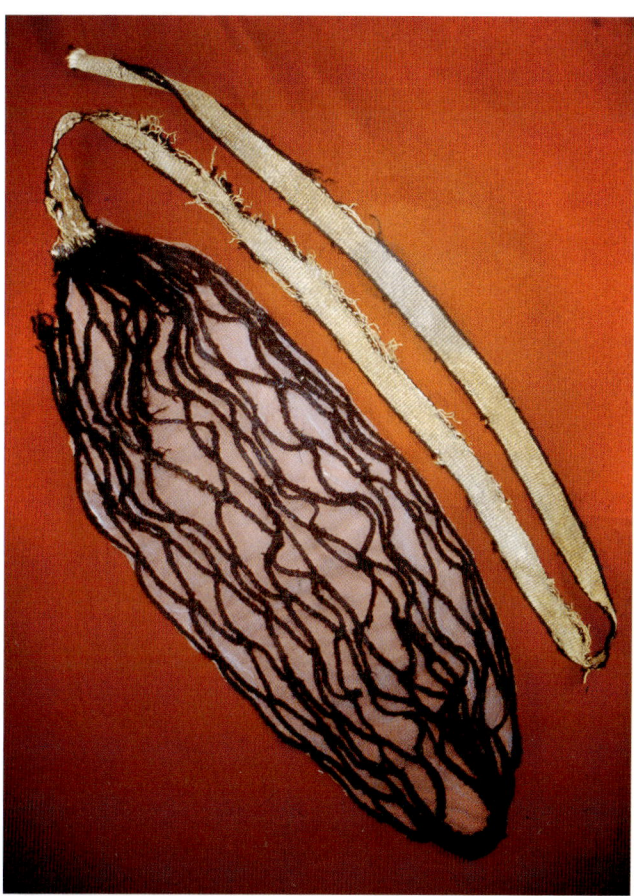

INCL 96. Photo: Lena bjerregaard.

Inventory Number: INCL 96

Item	Carrying net
Material	Camelid fiber and human hair
Ply and diameter	Braiding: 3S, 3 mm
	Band: warp: 2S, 1.5mm
	Weft: 2S (× 3), 2mm
Threads per cm	Band: 20 × 3
Technique	Braiding; warp faced plain-weave
Colors	Dark brown and beige
Size	Band: 58 × 4.5 cm
	Net: 90 cm

Description

A carrying net braided from strands of very coarse, dark brown camelid fiber (deck hair) and human hair. One end of the net has a handle measuring 10cm. This handle is formed over a wrapped core of camelid fiber yarns. At either end of the handle the camelid fiber yarns are divided into five strands of 12 yarns that are each braided by four. Every 8cm the five strands cross and inter-braid with one another to create a net with a mesh measuring 8 × 8cm. A long band has been sewn onto the other end of the net. This band has 0.5cm dark brown edges and is beige in the middle. When used, the band continued into the handle and the band was passed over the forehead or the shoulders with the net carried on the back. Similar carrying nets made of *cabuya* are still used in the region today.

CMA 839. Photo: Lena Bjerregaard.

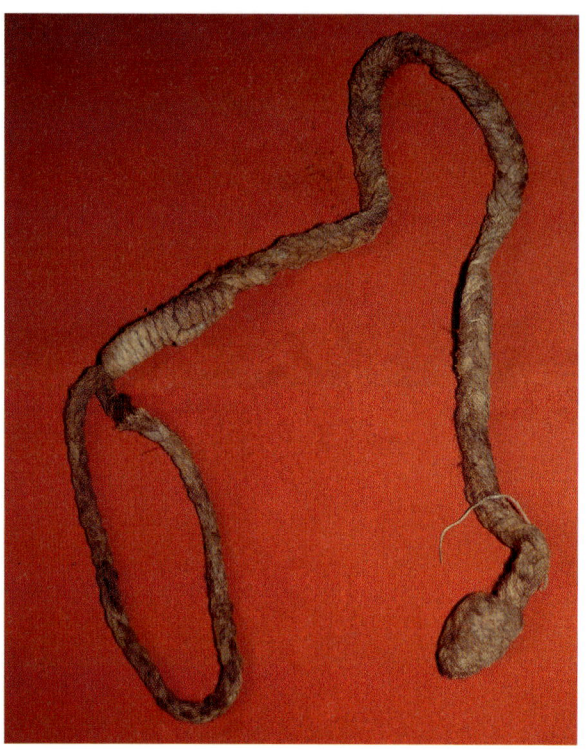

CMA 840. Photo: Lena Bjerregaard.

INVENTORY NUMBER: CMA 839

Item	Sling
Material	Plant fiber
Ply and diameter	S, 1-2mm
Threads per cm	–
Technique	Braiding
Colors	Natural beige
Size	97 × 5.5cm (at widest part). (18cm projectile-holder, 37 and 40cm braided cord on each side, 5cm loop.)

DESCRIPTION

Braided sling made of plant fiber. At one end of the sling is a finger loop 0.8mm wide, made of six individual warp pairs between each insertion of the weft. This warp-twining technique was carried out with loose warps and tied in a circle after completion. The loop is followed by 40cm of cord formed by a braid of five strings with a circumference of 2cm.

The cradle of the sling, which held the missile, consists of six flat 4-strand braids each one cm wide. These braids are attached to each other at irregular intervals (appearing as outer strings pulled from various neighbouring braids). Only one attachment string is intact.

At either side of the cradle is a 37cm-long cord braided with five strands. These cords become progressively narrower as the distance to the cradle increases and the last 12cm they are twisted into a 3Z plied string, which divides into two 2Z plied strings for the last 5cm. These two last strings are tied in a knot, forming a loop.

INVENTORY NUMBER: CMA 840

Item	Whip
Material	Plant fiber
Ply and diameter	Unspun
Threads per cm	–
Technique	Braiding; knotting

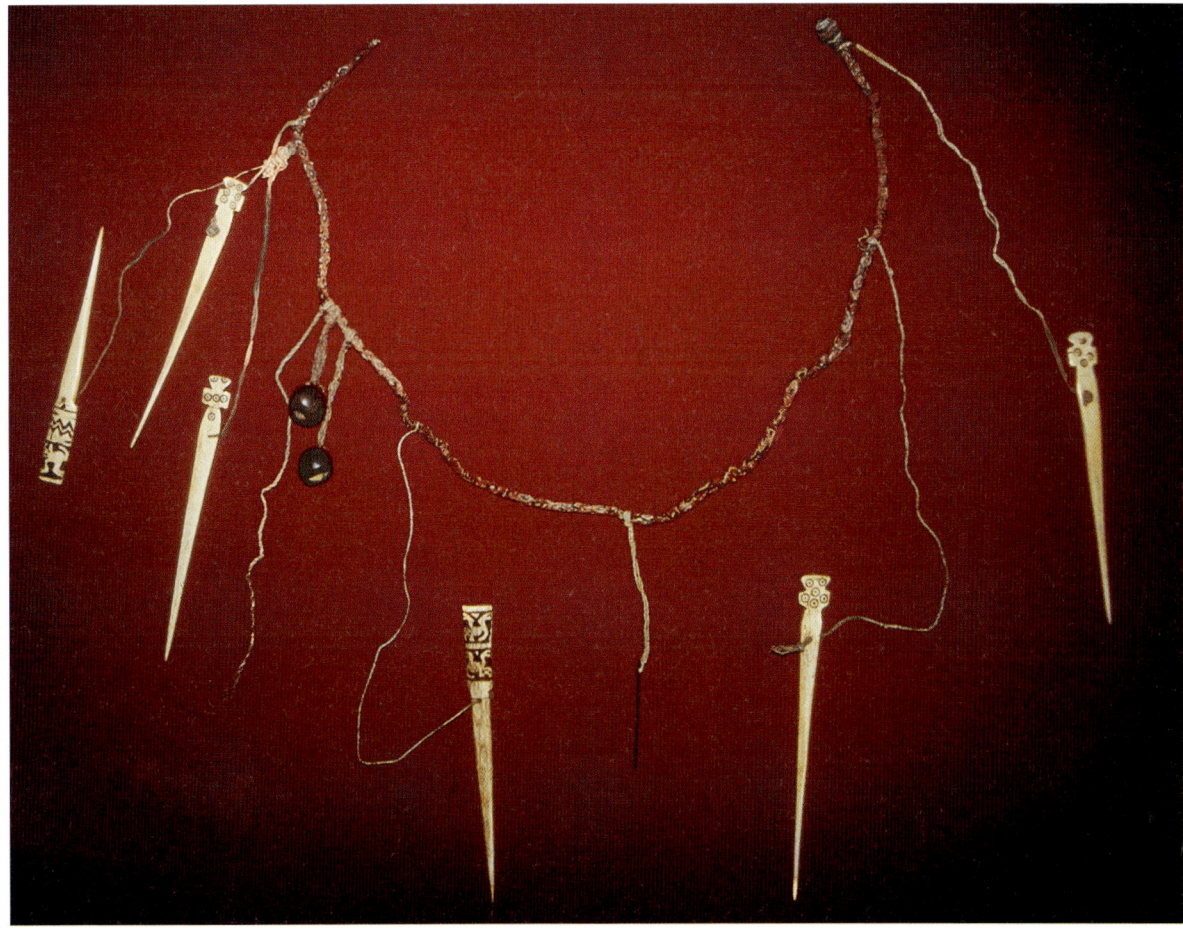

CMA 1795. Photo: Lena Bjerregaard.

Colors   Natural tan
Size   74cm long

DESCRIPTION

A braided rope, possibly used as a whip, made of undyed plant fiber. At one end of the rope is a 16cm-long loop which served as a handle, braided from five strands to create a round cord. This is followed by 6.5cm of rope that ends where the two strands of the handle are tied together and tightly wrapped. The upper half of this wrapped area is separated in two parts. As the fibers emerge from this section they are divided into four strands and braided for another 47cm. The rope ends with a knot resembling the long knots of a khipu with six loops.

INVENTORY NUMBER: CMA 1795

Item	Tupu cord
Material	Camelid fiber, cotton, bone, plant material
Ply and diameter	Core: camelid fiber: 2Z, 0.4mm
	Spiralling foundation thread: cotton, 2S, 0.5-0.6mm
	Embroidery: camelid fiber: 2S, 0.6mm
Threads per cm	Spiralling: 8
	Embroidery: approx. 14
Technique	Wrapped cord with stem-stitch embroidery

CMA 1836. Photo: Lena Bjerregaard.

Colors   Core: dark red
              Spiralling: cream
              Embroidery: red, brown, white, yellow
Size   71.5cm (length) × 1.5cm (circumference)

DESCRIPTION

A *tupu* cord adorned with six bone needles decorated with felines and geometric designs (probably used for weaving pickup), two palm seeds and a cactus or *algarrobo* needle. The *tupu* cord was once attached to two *tupus* (dress pins), but these were removed by looters.[5]

The wrapped and embroidered cord has an "eye" or diamond pattern. One end of the cord is finished with an oval knob (circumference: 1.5 × 3cm), which is embroidered with stripes. The other knob is fragmented. No doubt strings were once attached to the knobs. The cord passed through holes in the *tupu* pins to secure the *tupu* cord to the pins.

The bone needles are attached to the *tupu* cord by 2Z cotton cord, and the palm seeds by 2S plant fiber threads.

Inventory Number: CMA 1836

Item	Inter-woven sticks
Material	Wood, camelid fiber, cotton and leather
Ply and diameter:	Camelid fiber: 2S, 0.7mm
	Cotton: 2S, 2mm
Threads per cm	16-26 × 2 sticks
Technique	Camelid fiber threads inter-woven with sticks
Colors	Camelid fiber: red, black, white and yellow
Size	31 × 27cm

Description

Camelid fiber threads inter-woven with 5mm-wide, flat sticks, forming a pattern of two diamonds. Along three edges of the piece (the fourth side is fragmented) the sticks are sewn together with cotton yarn. On two sides of the piece, between the cotton yarn and the camelid fiber, is a narrow (approx. 1cm wide) strip of leather. The diamond pattern is classically Inca.

The function of the object is uncertain – similar fragments housed in the Ethnologisches Museum in Berlin measure up to 50 by 60 cm.

Notes

1 J.H. Rowe 1979.
2 The cotton fibers of the tunic are not saturated, indicating that the pigments (probably mineral) were applied in a thick paste to the fabric (cf. Stone-Miller 1992).
3 Keith Muscutt, personal communication, 2001.
4 Chuspas, or bags for carrying coca leaves (used by men) were common diplomatic gifts conferred by Inka functionaries on *mitmaq* colonists or local lords (J.H. Rowe 1979, A.P. Rowe 1997).
5 The Laguna de los Cóndores *tupu* cords are among the few known Inka examples still attached to their associated *tupu* pins. A number of objects were suspended from the cords: palm seeds, cactus or *algarrobo* thorn needles, spondylus pendants, silver or bronze tweezers, bone weaving instruments and, in one case, Spanish colonial glass beads. Women used the pins, with the points facing upwards, to fasten their wrapped dresses, and the cord passed through holes in the pins and then was twisted around the pins and the *tupu* cord to secure them (A.P. Rowe 1997). A drawing by Felipe Guaman Poma de Ayala (see below) shows a woman wearing dress pins with a *tupu* cord and three pendants suspended between the pins.

Inka woman wearing dress pins with a *tupu* cord. (Guaman Poma, *Nueva corónica* [1615], GKS 2232 4°, p. 120. Credit: The Royal Library, Copenhagen)

Bibliography

Anthon, F. (1984): *Altindianische Textilkunst aus Peru*. A.Seemann Verlag, Leipzig.

Adorno, R., ed. (2001): *Guaman Poma and his Illustrated Chronicle from Colonial Peru*. Museum Tusculanum Press, Copenhagen.

Bjerregaard, L. (1978): *Techniques of Guatemalan Weaving*. Høst & Søn, Copenhagen.

— (2002): *Pre-Columbian Woven Treasures in the National Museum of Denmark*. Corpus Antiquitatum Americanensium/Nationalmuseet, Copenhagen.

— (2007): *Fistbraided pre-Columbian Bands from Peru in the Ethnologisches Museum, Berlin*. Textile Museum Journal, vols. 44–45

Briceño, Jesús and Keith Muscutt (2004): "Fardos funerarios Chachapoya en la Laguna Huayabamba". *Sian* 9/15: 6–7.

Boone, H.E., ed. (1996): *Andean Art at Dumbarton Oaks*, vol. 2. Dumbarton Oaks Research Library and Collections, Washington, DC.

Braun, B. ed. (1995): *Arts of the Amazon*. Thames and Hudson, New York.

Burger, R.L. (1992): *Chavin and the Origins of Andean Civilization*. Thames and Hudson, New York.

Cahlander, A. (1978): "Bolivian Tubular Edging". *The Weaver's Journal*.

— (1980): *Sling Braiding of the Andes*. Colorado Fiber Center, Boulder.

de la Calancha, A. ([1638] 1974): *Corónica Moralizada del Orden de San Augustín en el Perú*. I. Prado Pastor, ed. Lima

Castillo, L.J. (2000): "La Presencia de Wari en San José de Moro". *Boletín de Arqueología PUCP* 4: 143–180.

Cieza de León, P. ([1553] 1862): *Primera Parte de la Crónica del Perú*. Biblioteca de Autores Españoles, 2 vols., Madrid.

— ([1553] 1959): *The Incas*. Harriet de Onis, translator, V. von Hagen, ed. University of Oklahoma Press, Norman.

Church, W. (1994): "Early Occupations at Gran Pajatén, Peru". *Andean Past* 4: 281–318.

— (1999): "Loving it to Death: The Gran Pajatén Predicament". *The George Wright Forum* 16/4: 16–27.

Conklin, W.J. (1971): "Chavin Textiles and the Origins of Peruvian Weaving". *Textile Museum Journal* 3/2: 13–19.

— (1996): "Huari Tunics". *Andean Art at Dumbarton Oaks*, Vol. 2, E.H. Boone, ed.: 375–398. Dumbarton Oaks Research Library and Collection, Washington, DC.

Easby, E. (1966): "Conservation of a Unique Peruvian Fabric". *Brooklyn Museum Annual* VII: 65–73.

Eisleb, D. and R. Strelow (1964): "Altperuanische kelim-gewebe aus den Sammlungen des Berliner Museums für Völkerkunde". *Baessler Archiv* 12: 257–270.

— (1975–87): *Altperuanische Kulturen I–IV*. Museum für Völkerkunde, Berlin.

Ekroth-Edebo, M. (1988): *Peruanska Textiler – en teknisk undersökning*, Göteborgs Universitet, Institutionen för Kulturvård, Gothenburg.

Emery, I. (1966): *The Primary Structures of Fabrics*. The Textile Museum, Washington, DC.

Engelstad, H. (1990): "A Group of Grave Tablets from Pachacamac". *Nawpa Pacha* 24: 61–72.

— (1984): "Mythology, Religion, and Textile Arts on the Central Coast of Old Peru". *Folk* 26: 191–217.

— (1985): *Vævninger fra det gamle Peru*. Nationalmuseet, Copenhagen.

Espinoza Soriano, W. (1967): "Los señoríos étnicos de Chachapoyas y la alianza hispano-chacha". *Revista Histórica* 30: 224–333.

Fernández López, A. (2002): "Análisis del Material Textil [de los Pinchudos]". *Sian* 8/12: 16–17.

Garcilaso de la Vega, El Inca (1966 [1609]): *Royal Commentaries of the Incas and General History of Peru*. Harold Livermore, translator. University of Texas Press, Austin.

Gohl, E.P.G. and L.D. Vilensky (1983): *Textile Science*. Longman Cheshire, Melbourne.

Grieder, T. (1978): *The Art and Archaeology of Pashash*. University of Texas Press, Austin.

Guaman Poma de Ayala, Felipe [1615] 2001: *El primer nueva corónica y buen gobierno*, The Royal Library, Copenhagen, GKS 2232 4°; complete facsimile on the internet: www.kb.dk/elib/mss/poma

Guillén, S. (n.d. a [1998]): *Arqueología de emergencia: Inventario, catalogación y conservación de los materiales arqueológicos de los mausoleos de la Laguna de los Cóndores*. Report submitted to the Instituto Nacional de Cultura, Lima.

— (n.d. b [1999]): *Evaluación y delimitación del sitio arqueológico Llaqtacocha*. Report submitted to the Instituto Nacional de Cultura, Lima.

— (2002): "The Mummies of the Laguna de los Cóndores". *Chachapoyas: The Lost Kingdom*. E. González and R. León, eds.: 345–387. AFP Integra, Lima.

von Hagen, A. (2000): "Nueva iconografía Chachapoya de la Laguna de los Cóndores". *Iconos* 4/2: 8–17.

— (2002a): *Los Chachapoya y la Laguna de los Cóndores*. Biblos, Lima.

— (2002b): "Chachapoya Iconography and Society at Laguna de los Cóndores", Peru. *Andean Archaeology 2: Art, Landscape and Society*, H. Silverman and W. H. Isbell, eds.: 137–155. Plenum, New York.

— (2002c): "People of the Clouds". *Chachapoyas: The Lost Kingdom*. E. González and R. León, eds.: 24–261. AFP Integra, Lima.

— (2004): "Plumas para el Rey: Cazadores de aves en la Laguna de los Cóndores". *Sian* 9/15: 24–25.

von Hagen, A. and S. Guillén (1998): "Tombs with a View". *Archaeology* 51/2: 48–54.

d'Harcourt, R. (1975): *Textiles of Ancient Peru and their Techniques*. University of Washington Press, Seattle.

Herrmann, B. and R-D. Meyer (1993): "Südamerikanische Mumien aus vorspanischer Zeit". *Neue Folge* 58, Museum für Völkerkunde, Berlin.

Isacsson, S.E. (1994): "Man of Fiber: The Paracas Fabrics in the Native Tradition of Western South America". *Acta Americana*, 2/2: 27–41, Svenska Amerikanist-selskabet, Uppsala Universitet, Uppsala.

Isbell, William H. (1997): *Mummies and Mortuary Monuments: A Postprocessual Prehistory of Central Andean Social Organization*. University of Texas Press, Austin.

Izaguirre, B. (1923): *Historia de las Misiones Franciscanas y Narración de los Progresos de la Geografía en el Oriente del Perú, 1619–1921*. Talleres Tipográficos de la Penitenciaría, Lima.

Jacobsen, J.; J.B. Jorgensen; L. Kempfner Jorgensen and I. Schjellerup (1987): "'Cazadores de cabezas' en Sitios pre-Inca de Chachapoyas, Amazonas". *Revista del Museo Nacional* 48: 139–185.

Jimenez Días, M.J. (2002): "Una 'Reliquia' Inca de los inicios de la Colonia: El uncu del Museo de America, Madrid". *Anales 10*, Museo de America, Madrid.

King, M.E. (1956): "A Preliminary Study of a Shaped Textile from Peru". *Workshop Notes* 13, The Textile Museum, Washington, DC.

— (1968): "Some new Paracas Textile Techniques from Ocucaje, Peru". *Verhandlungen des XXXVIII internationalen amerikanischen Kongresses*, Stuttgart-München, Band I: 369–377.

Kubler, G. (1975): *The Art and Architecture of Ancient America: The Mexican/Maya and Andean Peoples*. Penguin Books, Harmondsworth.

de Lavalle, J.A. and R. de Lavalle de Cárdenas (1999): *Tejidos Milenarios del Perú*. AFP Integra, Lima.

Lerche, P. (1995): *Los Chachapoya y los símbolos de su historia*. Ediciones y Servicios Gráficos César Gayoso, Lima.

— (1999): "A Grave Case of Robbery". *Geographical* 71/5: 18–23.

Menzel, D. (1959): "The Inca Occupation of the South Coast of Peru". *Southwestern Journal of Anthropology* 15: 125–142.

— (1976): *Pottery Style and Society in Ancient Peru: Art as a Mirror of History in the Ica Valley, 1350–1570*. University of California Press, Berkeley.

Montell, G. (1929): *Dress and Ornament in Ancient Peru*. Elanders, Gothenburg.

Muscutt, K. (1998): *Warriors of the Clouds: A Lost Civilization in the Upper Amazon of Peru*. University of New Mexico Press, Albuquerque.

O'Neale, L.M. (1934): "Peruvian Needleknitting". *American Anthropologist* 36: 405–431.

Onuki, Y. (1997): "Ocho Tumbas Especiales de Kuntur Wasi". *Boletín de Arqueología PUCP* 1: 79–114.

Paul, A. (1979): *Paracas Textiles*. Göteborgs Etnografiska Museum, Gothenburg.

Polo de Ondegardo, J. (1916 [1571]): *Los errores y supersticiones de los indios, sacadas del tratado y averigación que hizó el licenciado Polo*. Colección de libros y documentos referentes a la historia del Perú, vol. 4, Lima.

ProAvesPerú (n.d. [2003]): *Avifauna y conservación de los Bosques de Leymebamba. Informe General*. Report submitted to the Museo Leymebamba, Leymebamba.

Reeves, P. (1968): "Conservation of a Peruvian Paracas Necropolis Mantle". *Curator* XI: 21–25.

Reichlen, H. and P. Reichlen (1950): "Recherches archéologiques dans les Andes du haut Utcubamba". *Journal de la Société des Américanistes, nouvelle série* 34: 219–250.

Rowe, A.P. (1971): "Interlocking Warp and Weft in the Nasca 2 Style". *Textile Museum Journal* 3/3l: 67–78.

— (1977): *Warp Patterned Weaves of the Andes*. The Textile Museum, Washington, DC.

— (1978): "Technical Features of Inca Tapestry Tunics". *Textile Museum Journal* 17: 5–28.

— (1984): *Costumes and Featherwork of the Lords of Chimor: Textiles from Peru's North Coast*. The Textile Museum, Washington, DC.

— (1992): "Provincial Inka Tunics of the South Coast of Peru". *Textile Museum Journal* 31: 5–51.

— (1997): "Inca Weaving and Costume". *The Textile Museum Journal* 34/35: 5–54.

Rowe, A.P. and J.H. Rowe (1996): "Inca Tunics". *Andean Art at Dumbarton Oaks*, Vol. 2. E.H. Boone, ed.: 453–466. Dumbarton Oaks Research Library and Collections, Washington, DC.

Rowe, J.H. (1979): "Standardization in Inka Tapestry Tunics". *The Junius B. Bird Pre-Columbian Textile Conference, May 19th and 20th, 1973*, A.P. Rowe, E. Benson and A.-L Schaffer, eds.: 239–264. The Textile Museum and Dumbarton Oaks, Washington, DC.

— (1982): "Inca Policies and Institutions Relating to the Cultural Unification of the Empire". *The Inca and Aztec States, 1400–1800*, G.A. Collier, R.I. Rosaldo and J.D. Wirth, eds.: 83–118. Academic Press, New York.

Ruiz Estrada, A. (n.d. [1972]): "La alfarería de Cuelap: Tradición y cambio". B.A. thesis, Universidad Nacional Mayor de San Marcos, Lima.

Salomon, F. (2002): "Patrimonial Khipus in a Modern Peruvian Village: An Introduction to the 'Quipocamayos' of Tupicocha, Huarochiri". *Narrative Threads: Exploration of Narrativity in Andean Knotted-String Records*, J. Quilter and G. Urton, eds.: 293–319. University of Texas Press, Austin.

Schjellerup, I. (1996): "Los Idolos de Agua Santa, Distrito de Chumuch, Provincia de Celendín, Cajamarca". *Revista del Museo de Arqueología e Historia* 6: 221–230.

— (1997): *Incas and Spaniards in the Conquest of Chachapoyas. Archaeological and Ethnohistorical Research in the Northeastern Andes of Peru*. GOTARC, series B, Gothenburg Archaeological Theses, 7. Göteborg University, Gothenburg.

Seiler-Baldinger, A. (1994): *Textiles: A Classification of Techniques*. Smithsonian Institution Press, Washington, DC.

Shady, R. and E. Rosas (1977): "El Horizonte Medio en Chota: prestigio de la cultura Cajamarca y su relación con el 'Imperio Wari'". *Arqueológicas* 16: 1–75.

Sherbondy, J. (1992): "Water Ideology in Inca Ethnogenesis". *Andean Cosmologies through Time*, Robert V.H. Dover, Katharina Seibold and John H. McDowell, eds.: 46–66. Indiana University Press, Bloomington

Shimada, I. (1991): *Pachacamac Archaeology: Retrospect and Prospect*. The University Museum of Archaeology and Anthropology, University of Pennsylvania, Philadelphia.

van Stan, I. (1967): *Textiles from Beneath the Temple of Pachacamac, Peru: A Part of the Uhle Collection of the University Museum, University of Pennsylvania*. Museum Monographs 7. The University of Pennsylvania, Philadelphia.

Steward, J.H. and A. Métraux (1948): "Tribes of the Peruvian and Ecuadorian Montaña". *Handbook of South American Indians*, Vol. 3, J.H. Steward, ed.: 535–656. Smithsonian Institution, Bureau of American Ethnology, Washington, DC.

Stone-Miller, R. (1992): *To Weave for the Sun: Andean Textiles in the Museum of Fine Arts, Boston*. Museum of Fine Arts, Boston.

Strelow, R. (1996): "Gewebe mit unterbrochenen Ketten aus dem Vorspanischen Peru". *Neue Folge* 61, Abteilung

Amerikanische Archaeologie X, Museum für Völkerkunde, Berlin.

Susanibar Cruz, D. (n.d. [2003]): *Identificación y Determinación de una Muestra Arqueológica Compuesta por Plumas Procedentes del Museo Leymebamba, Amazonas, Perú*. Report Submitted to the Museo Leymebamba, Leymebamba.

Taylor, G. (1996): "La tradición oral quechua de Chachapoyas". Travaux de l'Institut Français d'Études Andines, vol. 95. IFEA, Lima.

Uhle, M. (1991 [1903]): *Pachacamac, a Reprint of the 1903 Edition by Max Uhle*. The University Museum of Archaeology and Anthropology, University of Pennsylvania, Philadelphia.

Urton, G. (1994): "A New Twist in an Old Yarn: Variation in Knot Directionality in the Inka Khipus". *Bessler Archiv, Neue Folge*, Band XLII: 271–303.

— (2001): "A Calendrical and Demographic Tomb Text from Northern Peru". *Latin American Antiquity* 12/2: 127–147.

— (2003): *Quipu*. Museo Chileno de Arte Precolombino, Universidad de Harvard.

Villagómez, Pedro (1919 [1649]): *Carta pastoral de exortación e instrucción contra las idolatrías de los indios del arzobispado de Lima*. Colección de libros y documentos referentes a la historia del Perú, vol. 12, Lima.

Watanabe, S. (2001): "Wari y Cajamarca". *Boletín de Arqueología PUCP* 5: 531–542.

The Authors

Lena Bjerregaard, M.A., is a textile conservator and works at Ethnologisches Museum, Berlin, where she is responsible for their large collection of pre-Colombian textiles. She wrote her dissertation on the collection of pre-Colombian textiles in Nationalmuseet, Copenhagen, published under the title: *Pre-Colombian Woven Treasures in the National Museum of Denmark*. She has also written a book on contemporary weaving techniques in Guatemala, and various articles on pre-Colombian textiles. The present book is based on the research work and analyses she conducted in 2001 of the Laguna de los Condores textiles in Leymebamba.

Sonia Guillén, Ph.D. Bioanthropologist. Professor at Universidad Católica del Peru. She is director of Centro Mallqui, an NGO dedicated to the conservation and study of archaeological material with special emphasis in human remains. Conducted in 1997 the salvage project that recovered the mummies and artefacts from the site Laguna de los Cóndores.

Adriana von Hagen writes on the archaeology of Peru where she is currently studying the Chachapoya and their interaction with the Incas. She is the author, with Craig Morris, of *Cities of the Ancient Andes*, *The Inka Empire and its Andean Origins* and *The Incas* (forthcoming).

Inge R. Schjellerup, Dr.h.c., Fil.dr., anthropologist, archaeologist, associated to the National Museum of Denmark, Universidad de Trujillo and Universidad Antenor Orrega, Peru; has directed interdisciplinary projects (archaeology, ethnohistory, botany and geography) in the Ceja de Montaña in north-eastern Peru since 1979. She is a specialist on the Chachapoya and the Inka cultures, with emphasis on settlement patterns and pre-Columbian agriculture. She has organized many symposiums and published several books and articles. The video "Behind the Ceja de Selva" is based on her work.

Gary Urton is Dumbarton Oaks Professor of Pre-Columbian Studies in the Archaeology Program, Department of Anthropology, Harvard University. His books include *At the Crossroads of the Earth and the Sky: An Andean Cosmology* (1981), *The History of a Myth: Pacariqtambo and the Origin of the Inkas* (1990), *The Social Life of Numbers: A Quechua Ontology of Numbers and Philosophy of Arithmetic* (1997), *Inca Myths* (2000) and *Signs of the Inka Khipu: Binary Coding in the Andean Knotted-String Records* (2003). He has also edited or co-edited numerous volumes on Inka civilization and Quechua culture in the Andes. He has been Director of the Khipu Database project at Harvard University since 2002.